TAROT FOR BEGINNERS

Master the Art of Psychic Tarot Reading, Learn the Secrets to Understanding Tarot Cards and Their Meanings, Common Tarot Spreads, Major Arcana, Minor Arcana, Become More Intuitive & Skilled, Learn the History, Symbolism and Divination of Tarot Reading

Shelly O'Bryan

Copyright 2019 by Shelly O'Bryan - All rights reserved.

No part of this book may be reproduced or transmitted in any form or by any means, electronic or mechanical, including photocopying, recording or by any information storage and retrieval system without written permission of the publisher, except for the inclusion of brief quotations in a review.

This content is provided with the sole purpose of providing relevant information on a specific topic for which every reasonable effort has been made to ensure that it is both accurate and reasonable. Nevertheless, by purchasing this content you consent to the fact that the author, as well as the publisher, are in no way experts on the topics contained herein, regardless of any claims as such that may be made within. As such, any suggestions or recommendations that are made within are done so purely for entertainment value. It is recommended that you always consult a professional prior to undertaking any of the advice or techniques discussed within.

This is a legally binding declaration that is considered both valid and fair by both the Committee of Publishers Association and the American Bar Association and should be considered as legally binding within the United States.

The reproduction, transmission, and duplication of any of the content found herein, including any specific or extended information will be done as an illegal act regardless of the end form the information ultimately takes. This includes copied versions of the work both physical, digital and audio unless express consent of the Publisher is provided beforehand. Any additional rights reserved.

Furthermore, the information that can be found within the pages described forthwith shall be considered both accurate and truthful when it comes to the recounting of facts. As such, any use, correct or incorrect, of the provided information will render the Publisher free of responsibility as to the actions taken outside of their direct purview. Regardless, there are zero scenarios where the original author or the Publisher can be deemed liable in any fashion for any damages or hardships that may result from any of the information discussed herein.

Additionally, the information in the following pages is intended only for informational purposes and should thus be thought of as universal. As befitting its nature, it is presented without assurance regarding its prolonged validity or interim quality. Trademarks that are mentioned are done without written consent and can in no way be considered an endorsement from the trademark holder.

TABLE OF CONTENTS

Introduction 1
Chapter 1 *What Is Tarot? The History And New Renaissance* 3
Chapter 2 *Tarot 101-Getting Started* 7
Chapter 3 *The Major Arcana* 12
Chapter 4 *Intro To The Minor Arcana* 73
Chapter 5 *Minor Arcana Number Card Relationships* 77
Chapter 6 *Minor Arcana Court Card Relationships* 80
Chapter 7 *Techniques For Reading Tarot* 83
Conclusion 95
Description 97

INTRODUCTION

Have you ever wanted to know what Tarot is all about? Maybe there are people in your life that practice Tarot and you want to learn more about it before diving in yourself. Many people are drawn to Tarot because of the air of mystery that surrounds it. Associated with fortune telling and the occult, Tarot comes with certain negative connotations. You might have heard that you should only have a Tarot deck in your possession if it was gifted to you, or that what you see in the cards will physically manifest in your life. We can thank pop culture and religion for warping the Tarot's intentions. Forget everything that you think you know about Tarot.

What started as a hand painted card game in Italy has evolved into a massive market catering to those seeking entertainment and tools for creating a deeper connection to our inner selves. Anyone can use Tarot cards, and with some practice, you can learn to understand each card on its own and in relation to the other cards. In a nutshell, all Tarot decks have 78 cards that are comprised of 22 Major Arcana cards and 56 Minor Arcana cards. Arcana can be translated as mystery, hidden, or secrets. In this book, we will delve into each card of the Major Arcana which are emblematic and represent life lessons and karmic influences in our lives. We will also explore the Minor Arcana and the way they relate to what's happening in our daily lives.

Because Tarot allows us to tap into our psyche's the cards can act as a sort of spiritual guide for us to develop further understanding and connection in our lives. Developing a sense of connection with your Tarot cards is a crucial step in the intuition and understanding that you'll develop when using them. We will explore ways to develop personal connections to each card and techniques for practicing how to perform readings for ourselves and others. Each of the Major Arcana descriptions contain potential references to questions that are being asked of the cards. This can help you learn to associate the type of question being asked to the representation given in the cards. As with anything that we want to be successful with, Tarot requires patience and practice.

When first learning how to read Tarot cards, it's important that you keep an objective point of view and understand that it's okay to play with them if it's done respectfully. Once you've got a basic understanding of each card or Suit, start practicing reading them in the Reversed, or Upside-down positions. No matter how long you may have been using Tarot, you will always find new ways of interpreting cards and achieve insights that are only possible through time and experience. Remember to keep things positive even when pulling cards that offer troubling contemplation as we are the masters of our own lives and we create our own paths based on the choices we make.

CHAPTER 1

What Is Tarot? The History And New Renaissance

What is Tarot?

It's helpful to think of the Tarot as a symbolic map of consciousness. This map contains our journey through life in all ways be it practical or spiritual. Reading Tarot cards is a way of divining guidance and wisdom through the way that we lay or spread them out. Their placement and the way they relate to the other cards near them are how we interpret the messages they contain.

Tarot cards are meant to provide insight into our lives and reveal what we may already know on a subconscious level. This means that you don't have to have psychic abilities to read Tarot cards. However, the level of clairvoyance of the reader will dictate the type of reading that one will get. One person usually reads for another, but it's possible to read for ourselves.

It's wise to remember that the cards themselves are not oracles. They do not reveal a future that is lying in wait for us, but rather we can use them to create the future we want. It's that revelation that the cards can hold that draws us to the Tarot. The Mystery and Lore surrounding the cards keep some people away, for fear of negative consequence, but others seek to understand them on a deeper level.

While most Tarot Readers understand that instructional books on the subject serve as guidelines and give us basic definitions, it's the personal practice by each of us that develops a style, technique, and deeper knowledge. It's important to keep in mind that the cards themselves do not contain any certain truth but that they serve as our mirrors and even windows that we can see a higher truth through. Every person can access this information when they bring intuition and sensitivity to their approach.

History of the Tarot

Where did Tarot come from, and what was its original intention? Most versions regarding the origin of the Tarot claim they began as hand-painted cards used in taverns for fun during the Renaissance by Italian nobles. This card came mirrors the game we know as Bridge. The Tarot has morphed over the ages into modern day decks and art that we have now. However, much of the Tarot story remains unknown. This is because many perspectives such as those of wise women who read cards in their homes were never passed along in books and material available to the public. Much knowledge has been passed down orally over the years. There is some history that point to the Tarot being much, much older than the Renaissance.

It's much easier to view the history of Tarot as an evolving timeline. Most history books point to the early 1400s as the time when the first decks appeared but it wasn't until the mid to late 1600's that The Marseille Tarot spread over Europe. Between this time and into the early 1900's occultists studied and morphed Tarot into being used for Divination. In the 1960s and '70s Tarot grew in popularity all over the globe and hundreds of new decks were created. The Rider Waite Smith that contains some of the most universally recognized illustrations in the Tarot. This deck was published in the early '70s by U.S. Games Systems. By the 90's many of the Pagan and Wiccan symbols were traded for traditional Christian symbolism.

In Europe, engraved stencils created by master paper producers were handed down over generations creating fundamental iconography of the Tarot. In the late 18th and 19th centuries, Tarot spread all over Europe as a card game. Before the printing dynasties came about, most of the general public played Tarot using flimsy paper, meant to be discarded, printed with wood block stamps.

The French Marseille Tarot is arguably the most successful and eventually became the point of reference for card players and manufacturers to come. Still considered an excellent deck for beginners, the Marseille Tarot seems to have details that will pop out at you even after you're familiar with the deck. In a minimalistic way, the cards maintain a consistent structure throughout. The minor pips or cards (1-10) are simply just a symbol repeated as many times as the card represents. For example, the 5 of Cups would have 5 actual cups and nothing else. In the Minor Arcana section of this book, we will explore the Marseille Tarot representations. This can be helpful in your learning journey as it will help you focus on the Major Arcana representations and the relationships of the minor cards.

In the mid-19th century, the Tarot was associated with planets, elements, zodiac signs, the Kabbalah, and alchemical symbology. Eliphas Levi and the assertions of others during this time created the connection between the Tarot and Egypt, divinatory powers, and antiquity. Cartomancy, divination using cards, grew in popularity and in mystery during this time. However, many are still drawn to the Marseille deck, especially beginners to Tarot, because it's the oldest *complete* deck. The images it uses are archetypes from our earliest recorded history. Those images contain heroic or serious primeval characters. The 22 allegorical images are associated with the human journey.

It's quite possible in present times to find a deck with illustrations relating to virtually anything we'd like. These are almost all based off a mix between the Marseille deck and the more recent Rider Waite Smith Tarot deck. The Rider Waite Smith decks were made for fortune telling and they represent the first time the Minor Arcana cards had illustrations. Pamela Coleman Smith's images in this deck set the bar for all the illustrations that followed. There are revisionist decks such as the Morgan-Greer and post-modern decks from those such as Starchild Tarot that are all worthy of looking into.

Tarot for Today's World

You may have noticed an increase in interest surrounding Tarot. It seems as if we are currently experiencing a sort of Tarot revival where Tarot readings are being performed via live video feeds online, Tarot Clubs are meeting up in public spaces to hold readings and fellowship with like minded people. What started out as a more mystical practice that helped form the works of many artists and philosophers before us, is now more of an insight into our current lives. Card interpretations can be given without the air of mystery or perceived implications. By removing the smoke and mirrors that have disguised Tarot for to long it is being opened to new audiences that can express it as more of a creative act rather than a metaphysical one. This ability to creatively read a story that the cards present and apply it to certain aspects of our lives is quite attractive. This pull is partly because it's all about us. No one else can truly understand what the cards mean to you on a personal level.

If you've never had your Tarot cards read, start there. You should be able to achieve this quite easily if you are willing to have a reading performed online or if you know of someone in your circle that has a Tarot deck. You can just pull one card, or find out your Birth Cards, or pose a question that you need insight on. Keep in mind that there is still a certain stigma that comes with the Tarot. Many followers of religion still warn against the idea of being able to control our own fates and rejecting God's creation and care over all life. Some leaders in religion are still creating fear around the Tarot by saying its use will attract demons and evil spirits. Even with the negativity that still surrounds the Tarot, many young people are drawn to embrace the mystic. As older generations sought consolation and order to their lives through religion, many people now are finding a sense of control through Tarot.

For many, the meditative practice of reading Tarot cards is in and of itself a reason to continue doing it. Handing over major life dilemmas and decisions to the ancient illustrations found in the Tarot can be both comforting and insightful during times where guidance is needed.

CHAPTER 2

Tarot 101-Getting Started

Now that you're ready to get a Tarot deck and begin the learning process, the first thing you must do is find your own Tarot deck and make it your own. You can then start to develop a personal connection with those cards and build a foundation that will provide you with guidance and insight for years to come.

- **Choosing a Tarot Deck**

Because there are so many Tarot decks now available, it can be difficult when first deciding which deck to use. Don't worry about choosing the wrong deck, as anything that calls to you is going to the right fit. You aren't limited to just having one deck either, you can and probably will end up with multiple decks that you use for various reasons. Some will keep one deck private, and only use it when they are reading cards for themselves. Others will use one deck for everything. Most teachers of Tarot recommend that you find a deck that you resonate with and use it to practice and learn with. Once you are comfortable enough to perform readings for others, you will know if you require a new deck for that purpose or if the one you already have will work.

No matter which deck you end up choosing, having a sense of connection with it is crucial. Take your time and browse all the options available to you. If you find a deck and decide that you don't really have any relationship with the images, find a new deck. You're not held to any commitment with the Tarot. Once you locate a deck that you like, you'll want to clear the energies that might exist around it and cleanse the deck. If that sounds a little too metaphysical for you, think about as introducing yourself to the deck and starting fresh.

- **Sorting**

To begin, you will want to sort out your cards and pay attention to any energies that you might pick up from them. On a clean table or area, sort your cards out in front of you in order. Start with the

Major Arcana cards and then sort the Suits of the Minor Arcana. Take a brief look at each card while doing this. This is a way of ensuring that you have all the cards in your deck as well as taking note of the illustrations for the first time. When dealing with the Minor Arcana cards, sort the Suits by type and then by number. You start with sorting in order from Ace through Ten followed by the Page, the Knight, the Queen, and finally the King card.

For the purposes of learning, you may want to sort your cards into the Major Arcana and the Minor Arcana and put one or the other away in the place you dedicate for storage. When we focus on either one of these specifically, we allow space for further insight and development with that section. For example, it's quite common to start with the Minor Arcana and to develop a good sense of what each Suit, Number or Court card is telling us. It makes us focus solely on a limited number of cards so that we can use the repetition to build on our original thoughts and impressions.

- **Cleansing Energies**

Once you have looked at each individual card and have it sorted you can use a smudging wand such as sage or sweetgrass to clear any stored energy in the cards. This is particularly useful if you have cards that have been used before, but it's also a great starting point for new decks. At this point, you may want to meditate on the cards and visualize energy coming from you and moving towards and into the cards. If you're familiar with guided meditation or visualization techniques, you may want to use them to create a protective circle of while light that encompasses you and the cards. This can be a powerful cleansing and connection exercise.

There are energy cleansing techniques that are much more involved such as salt burials, moon bathing, or water clearing. If you feel your cards have any negative energies associated or clinging to them, take the time to perform a cleansing ritual with them. For beginners though, a simple sorting and pause in contemplation should suffice. It's recommended that you do some sort of energy clearing, however small, before performing any readings to concentrate on the questions at hand and the client.

- **Making the cards your Own**

When you are satisfied with the energy, pick them all up and shuffle them to impart your own energy into the cards. Continue shuffling and reshuffling any way you like to achieve this. Maybe you want to shuffle a certain lucky amount of times or randomly select cards to put on top or at the bottom of the deck. Whatever works for you will get your deck ready for its first use. When your deck is not being used, you should consider where you will store them. Many people find the box that they came in completely okay while others have a dedicated, specialized space just for them. Silk is associated with magical properties due to how it's created and is widely accepted as the fabric of choice when wrapping cards before placing in a box. While it's fine to do what feels right for you, keep in mind that Tarot is an ancient artform that deserves our respect and reverence.

Develop a Personal Connection

Now you are ready to work with your cards and develop a personal connection to them. This connection should be with every single card in the Tarot deck. You may choose to begin with the Minor Arcana and develop a sense of what each Suit represents. You may decide to start with the Major Arcana and develop an understanding with the illustrations found there. However, you go about learning the cards for the first time, you'll want to associate meaning to each one. You will begin to develop a relationship with your cards, which is why working with a deck you like and resonate with is so crucial. You're basically bonding with the deck and noting how you feel when using it.

You don't have to memorize the meaning of each card, only develop a basic sense of what the card represents at first. You will inherently acquire a sense of what they mean as you continue to work with them. Keep in mind that you will at one point want to express what they represent to other people so work on creating associations that are easily recognized, repeated, and deciphered. This should be fun for you, so if you feel that it's becoming too much information just take a step back and return when you are ready. You don't have to learn the whole deck right away; you can pull one card and sit with it until you feel ready to move on. Some people select only one card and meditate on it and learn everything they can from it for an entire month. This can take a very long time but if you are serious about using Tarot for deeper insight, it's a practice that is highly recommended. Remember that you can do this as you practice daily.

For now, any symbolism and representation that you find in each card are completely fine. Lay out all the cards and with a birds-eye-view take note of any patterns that emerge. Keep a journal of themes that the cards share and feelings that they give you. Refer to your journal throughout your learning to build upon your relationship with them. The interpretations of each card are only activated when you are interacting with them. When you have a need for the indications, you will be ready to find them and use them. Use this time you are spending bonding with your Tarot cards to develop your own opinions about them. The deck you chose essentially becomes an extension of your voice. Be honest with anyone that might approach you for a reading early on. Let me know that you can do it for fun but that they shouldn't take anything that comes across seriously as you are just learning. Remember, these meanings are hypothetical and not necessarily prophetic. You and the people you may do readings for are safe from harm.

Shuffling

Learn to Shuffle your Tarot deck. Unless it's very small, shuffling a deck can be difficult. This is because the cards are larger and thicker. There are many ways to successfully shuffle a deck- just keep in mind that if you are spreading them out and circulating them repeatedly that you do so on a clean surface where they will not be damaged. You can attempt to shuffle them like a regular playing card deck, or try shuffling half of them at a time, etc. You can cut them repeatedly, or have your client cut them. The goal is to have the cards be completely randomized while you're contemplating the questions being asked. This is the difference between getting a meaningful reading and not just random cards to interpret.

When you are performing a reading for someone else, consider letting them shuffle the deck so that they can get in tune with their energies. If that's not something you're comfortable with, that's okay! Maybe you can compromise by letting them cut the deck as many times as they want to without ever fully handling your cards.

Discover where your boundaries are regarding your cards and demand they be respected.

You can always pick up a spread and reshuffle the deck and re-spread them. If you are not connecting with the person asking the questions, or you are not in a headspace to interpret the cards you'll find that reading the Tarot cards is hard to do. Clear the energy around you and on your cards and begin again. You do not have to forcefully pull meaning out of the cards. This should take exertion on your part as the cards will provide the insight you are looking for just by sight. You can develop intuitive reading quickly through practice!

CHAPTER 3

The Major Arcana

The cards of the Major Arcana are numbered as zero through 21. The cards align with the journey of Life and represent passages that we all must take. Though we all face the milestones depicted in the Major Arcana, we do so at different times and with different meanings. Some things will be recurring and phases and it's important to remember that there is no one point of beginning or end.

The Major Arcana be a journey that starts with the Fool and ends with the World card, that once completed starts again. These cards build upon each other and connect in various and evolving ways. The following descriptions are based on the traditional illustrations accompanied by each of the Major Arcana. Remember to develop your own sense of what each card represents and take note of these things in a journal.

The Fool

The Fool is the first card and the last card in the Major Arcana of the Tarot and is not assigned a number. Commonly referred to as the "Zero" card, there is no actual number, even zero, on the card itself. The Fool is known as the start of the journey, a free spirit, and sometimes it has been used as a wild card that is able to be played at any time. He is known for plunging headfirst into situations with no thought or respect for limits and boundaries. The Fool is usually depicted as a beggar or jester but is also known as someone that is invisible to the crowd, a prince in disguise. The Fool does not care about what others may think of him or what he looks like.

He represents the freedom of all things and is pure potential. Enthusiasm and joy and spontaneity are his weapons. Mirroring the misery of the human condition, The Fool enters and exits on his own terms. The card seems to say to us that it's the essence of our spirit before we came into existence. The Fool is our complete potential in this world, all our talents, gifts, and qualities. Through the Fool, we realize that the only restraints and limits are the ones we impose on ourselves.

The Fool teaches us that every moment is a new one, and we can begin at every turn. He teaches us that we are protected and should not fear the wild recklessness. The Fool shows us to embrace those things that bring new chances, fresh air, and possibilities we thought unimaginable. The Fool is asking that we take his hand and leap without fear. The Fool is our possibilities, our sense of overwhelming potential.

He represents the very beginning but also the end. The genesis or representation of all possibility and everything that's come before that's led us here. Not to be a journey from birth to death, not an infant or newborn. Don't think of this literally. A journey to individuation, or enlightenment. A journey to know who you are. You can be the Fool many times of your life- at that great beginning.

Upright

The Fool can be interpreted as a completely fresh start and the beginning of something new. The card says to us that we can begin again and that we are full of potential. Also interpreted as finding new roads and pathways to travel while holding no detachment to responsibilities or worries.

In general, this card appearing in a reading shows something unexpected and completely new. This also indicates the need to take the time to look before you take the steps. Spiritual- New discoveries, spiritual journeys, new knowledge. Keep doing what is right for you and don't look at what others are doing.

- **Finance and Career**- it can indicate the time to move forward if there has been any thought of starting a new business or going for a new job. For something you are already working on it can mean new energy and fresh ideas. The Fool reminds us to work hard and you will get more than you expect. Be clever using the new chances and opportunities that are coming your way.
- **Love & Relationships**- The Fools asks us to let go of our fears and trust in our hearts. Indicating an

arrival of a fun-filled romance keep your eyes open for true love. Impulsive and carefree romance.
- **Health**- good and improving health but also being accident prone. If pulled for health, take care.

Reversed Reading

Interpreted as stagnancy. Being stuck and not having the willingness to move or experience new things. This could be because of fear or feeling trapped, causing paralyzing and unmoving action in your life. Also thought to mean making negative choices and acting without thinking. Denying the truth. A new beginning that is blocked, difficulty seeing the world with fresh eyes. Reckless behavior.

Symbols for The Fool- Illustration breakdown

- **Bag** -on the shoulder representing experiences and lessons-both negative and positive. The experience that we all carry with us into the future.
- **Clothing**- sometimes the rags of a beggar, or the ornate jester the Fool will have extravagant and an unconventional personality that shines through all encounters and situation
- **Animal**- Instinct. Sometimes an irrational impulse that helps overcome dangers and obstacles. Sometimes self-defeating. Forces attempting to hold you back or push you into the unknown. Also, the deep loyalty of another.
- **Feather**- Red feathers indicate vitality, passion, and innocence

Keywords

Wandering, Adventure, Strangeness, Potential, Playful, Trickster, Originality, Risk, Learning, Spontaneity

Reversed Keywords

Carelessness, Risk, Lack of Hope, Arrogance

The Magician

The Number One card. The Magician is the first card in the Major Arcana. The only card that refers to the suits of the minor cards in the Major Arcana. Representing the power of creation using desire and willpower. Sometimes represented by mercury, the planet/God of smooth talkers and salesmen, Mercury was the God of Thieves, the Magician can be known as a trickster as well. This relates to the sleight of hand, the cleverness, and medicine man. The Magician reveals the raw, undirected, and undeveloped power of each element to us.

The Magician is known as an artist and craftsman admired for having powerful mental abilities, physical coordination, and great confidence. On the other hand, quick-change artist that is hard to trust as the truth may be confused. The Magicians real strength is being able to tackle any situation with ease because of their wealth of resources, improvisation, and guided imagination. The 4 elements in the form of the Magician's tools are at his disposal. He is directing the energy of virtue and light into the material realm. The Magician can manifest magic quickly, and their ambition is ever growing.

Use the power of the Magician to make yourself known to the Universe. We are conduits that bridge the spiritual and material planes. With the Magicians tools, we manifest. The Magician is telling you to manipulate, ignite, and challenge the world to achieve this manifestation. He reminds us that we have everything we need before us and that we will always receive everything that is required. The Magician is the power of intention, reminding us that we are unstoppable once we've claimed our self-power. He invites you to make magic with him.

The Magician urges us to use our will and intellect to make things happen. With focused attention and directing our will, all potential for success is at our fingertips. If we act with concentration and awareness we can benefit from our creative forces. When studying this card, or when you are pulling one card a day for guidance, the Magician indicates strong spiritual awareness and psychic abilities. Knowing that we have everything we need, if you are interested in using this awareness you will be surprised by the results you can achieve.

Upright

The Magician reveals to us new ideas. This is done so that we can verbalize and actualize those ideas. The union of that divine force above and that which is below is reflected in the Magician. This represents energy and the energetic creation of new things. He can indicate a time that you are inventive, charismatic, and persuasive. Because the Magician is also known as a trickster, if the card is meant to represent someone in your life be sure that they are genuine, and that magnetic connection is not a con.

- **Finance and career**- The Magician shows us a potential opportunity where your talent will be showcased, and extra money can be made. This could be a promotion, a new job, or consulting focused. It could be a good time for starting a new business venture or connections. Feeling self-assured and powerful it could be your finances are improving or that the opportunity for making extra money is very high when you pull the Magician. This card relates to speech and writing such as storytelling, public speaking, and sales. This could represent self, what you want to be, someone who was, is, or may be in your life.
- **Love-** Generally known as a positive card, the Magician represents a great time to meet someone new. This can mean a strong and easy love with your partner, and the end of the conflict with talking.
- **Health-** Representing strength, the Magician is known to represent getting well by trying alternative therapies, and experienced doctors. A sign of healing, if you will.

Reversed Reading

The Magician reversed can represent a lack of intelligence, an absence of training or education, and a lack of knowledge. This could mean not reaching anything through the actions you are taking. Communicating and articulating ideas to someone could be blocked. Do not be consumed with self-doubt. This card reversed also warns of someone in your life that you believe to be knowledgeable and trustworthy but is attempting to manipulate or use you.

Symbols for The Magician- Illustration breakdown

- **Infinity/Lemniscate**- Sometimes shown in the curves of their hat brim- the esoteric sign of infinity can also be seen just above the Magicians head. This is a representation of being able to turn every thought in each direction.
- **Wand**- Represented by a candle that's burning at both ends, the Magicians wand is raised towards the heavens, the ether, as the other hand points towards the Earth. This is the visual interpretation of divine IMMANENCE, connective heaven and Earth.
- **Tools**- On the Magicians table are found the four elements of earth, air, fire, and water represented in the four suits of the Tarot. Water and Knowledge are symbolized by a cup, Air and Courage are represented by a knife. The secrets of nature and the Earth element are found in the pentacle or coin symbol, and finally, the wand of ambition and passion represents the Fire element.
- **Table**- Sometimes shows with three legs representing the three worlds in which the Magician acts: physical, spiritual, and intellectual. This shows the plane of reality that the Magician manipulates using the tools.

Keywords

Talent, Energy, Determination, Power, Desire, Communication.

Reversed Keywords

Manipulation, Powerlessness, Greed, Weakness.

The High Priestess

The Number Two card. The High Priestess suggests possessing an inherent sense of good judgement and strong intuition. Representing serenity, wisdom, knowledge, and understanding, the High Priestess is the guardian of our subconscious and intuition. She tells us to pay attention to your senses, and signs from the Universe. Also thought to indicate a change in our lives and point to the unknown.

As the custodian of all knowledge, the High Priestess can understand the secrets in the sacred scroll that is on her lap. As the symbol of analysis, study, and research her gifts are in theory and abstraction, not practical applications. Linked to all the feminine aspects of the Divine. This card represents the knowledge inside of you, and your inner truth. She is thought to hold on to these secrets and reminds us that someday we will know their truth.

The High Priestess springs from deep wells of knowledge that reside inside of us. She contains the truth of our past, present, and future- essentially the book of us. She is the inner voice who responds when you seek an answer. She represents our intuition and subconscious and we are called to listen and trust her voice. Learn to decipher the communications we receive from her in symbols and impulse. When we trust in the guardian of our inner knowledge, we will not be led astray.

She is the card of inner knowledge that calls us to try something different and even move out of our comfort zones to become a better version of ourselves. She calls us to trust our own instincts and the signs that we feel and see.

Upright

The High Priestess reveals to us hidden secrets and knowledge of the occult. She is the keeper of moon magic and those feminine mysteries. When this card is pulled it can represent an unrevealed future and the hidden influences that are at work in our lives. A good indication that your life is changing, and a reminder to pay attention to our dreams and signs presenting themselves to us.

- o **Finance and career**- This card says that though we shouldn't expect sudden, new gains or income, our finances are safe and the investments we've made will be beneficial in the long-term. An indication of important information and/or opportunities that we will benefit from. The High Priestess can also represent that someone is not being completely honest with you, something is concealed from you regarding your finances and/or career.
- o **Love-** Thought to indicate a need to look deeper on your true self. This card is also thought to mean the need for taking some time out to do this. She represents being desired by more than one person around you.
- o **Health-** The High Priestess urges you to trust your instincts and body and through the power of intuition- listening to our bodies when we feel something may be

wrong. For women an indication of fertility and hormonal balance. With health, she reminds us to take care of ourselves physically.

Reversed Reading

When this card is interpreted in reverse it indicates that one is disconnected from their inner selves. This can mean a block regarding your Intuition. She can also represent missing important signs in our lives. The High Priestess reversed can indicate focusing on others' opinions and approval when she calls us to listen to that inner voice and be true to ourselves. Representing not taking the time to relax when we are so busy rushing around in our daily lives, and frantic, irrational behavior. Another reversed meaning is of a person deceiving you, and the ways we avoid the truth in a situation.

Symbols for The High Priestess- Illustration breakdown

- **Veil**-Fabric is traditionally embellished with pomegranates and palms. This veil prevents us from knowing what is seen beyond it, and the inaccessible knowledge that the High Priestess guards. The veil is the threshold of that hidden knowledge. The pomegranates are known to represent her ambition.
- **Headwear**- The tiara symbolizes contact with all three levels of existence; physical, spiritual, and intellectual. The headwear is also representative of the three phases of the moon. This crown of Isis indicates that she is a believe or magic.
- **Columns**- The High Priestess is typically depicted as sitting between two pillars known to be at Solomon's Temple. The right column, Jachin, is referred to as the Pillar of Establishment. The left column, Boaz, is referred to as the Pillar of Strength. Thought to represent the duality of nature, the negative and positive, and the masculine and feminine. As she is located between the two columns, she represents a responsibility to serve as a mediator between the depths of reality-she acts as the third pillar, or this path between.
- **Moon**- There is a crescent moon at her feet that is commonly depicted in visions of the Virgin Mary. This

indicates that the High Priestess has a complete grasp over emotion.
- **Scroll-** She is shown holding the book of knowledge, or the Torah. The scroll, or sometimes book, is shown neither being opened or closed.
- **Cross-** Denotes a connection to the seasons of the Earth and a connection to the Earth itself. The Cross is a focal point where all energies from Above and Below meet. A connection between the yin and yang, the black and white.

Keywords

Feminine, Mystery, Study, Introspection, Fertility, Inner Power, Understanding

Reversed Keywords

Blocked, Imbalance, Frustration, Undesired Attention, Fertility Issues

The Empress

The Number Three card. The Empress is associated with a strong maternal influence and is a great sign if you are seeking harmony in relationships or have the hope of starting a family. This maternal force represents the transformation of knowledge into action. She provides and creates life and supports and protects others. The Empress reflects authority, conviction, and strength.

Traditionally connected to pregnancy, this could mean a pregnancy of the body or the mind. She rules with the Emperor who reflects all the male aspects, and her femininity is complementary to him as she is more nurturing and emotional. She is the essence of femininity and creativity within us. She calls us to never doubt the power we must transform and manifest the world as we have imagined it.

The Empress encourages us on every step of our journeys. She is our greatest champion and we are safe within her arms. She lets us know that we are never without her touch as she will love us forever and listen to us. She sees the potential we have within us and we are entwined with her in the eternal fabric of life. She calls us to create extraordinary possibilities. She indicates a good time for starting a spiritual path and an ability to easily connect to higher powers who will lead you through your instincts.

Upright

The Empress reveals to us exposure to strong bouts of artistic and creative energies. This could be an addition to your immediate or extended family or a family of a close friend. Generally thought to be a very good sign for you and those around you. This card tells of a new beginning and the importance of being understanding and sensitive.

When this card is pulled it can indicate great luxury. A knowledge that anything is possible, and that creativity and growth are abundant. She allows us to know that the answer is "yes." She signifies a strong connection to our femininity such as nurturing, sensuality, and creative expression. She calls on us to connect with that feminine energy and create beauty in our lives.

Take a moment to reflect on all that surrounds us that we can offer gratitude for. Concentrate on this so that you can build on this energy and create more of it as abundance in your life. Venture out into nature and feel the energy of the Earth so that you can reach higher planes of consciousness.

- **Finance and career-** The Empress indicates prosperity and cash flow. This could be a good time to make investments or to trust your intuition and instincts. She reminds us to share with those in need and to inspire them with our passions. She shows us being rewarded for our efforts and completing our projects on time.
- **Love-** This card represents an excellent time for love and romance in both platonic and non-platonic relationships. Committed relationships become more loving and deeper while those looking may meet their special one sooner than later. Regarding Love, The Empress can indicate good sex, and as a symbol of motherhood, it means to take care to avoid unwanted pregnancies.
- **Health-** The Empress tells us to listen to our bodies. Allow yourself to rest and enjoy life. If you are trying for pregnancy, it is an excellent time.

Reversed Reading

This card reversed can indicate suppression of your feminine side and a need to embrace it so those energies can be balanced-this applies to both men and women. Upside down, the Empress can show a lack of growth in the area or situation in question. It could be that it is not a good time to move forward with any ideas or plans or that you could expect obstacles and challenges on your path. This could mean that your resources are scattered and that you are stifled as an artist. The reversed Empress translates to Infertility, though not specifically dealing with sexual fertility.

Symbols for The Empress- Illustration breakdown

- **The crown-** her crown is a symbol of the supremacy of intellect. A golden tiara that is thought to be the sun itself. The crown can be traditional or made from 12 stars. This signifies her connection to the mystical realm and the Earths cycles.
- **Throne-** The throne is thought to represent common thoughts and the Empress sitting on it expresses stability, and her capacity to rise above them.
- **Scepter-** The Empress' scepter shows a power that she has over the material world. This also expresses the combination of sensibility and sense.
- **Robe-** Her robe is sometimes shown without embellishments, but when there is a pattern, she is typically shown wearing a gown that has feminine symbols such as the pomegranate and other symbols of fertility.
- **Heart and Venus signs-** Expressing the Empress' qualities as a mother and her female nature.
- **Nature/Water-** The Empress is shown sitting in a lush, beautiful forest near a stream. This indicates her connection with life itself and Mother Earth. Drawing a sense of peace from the water and trees she is rejuvenated by nature's energy. The lushness represents her connection to the vital energies and the power of life.

Keywords

Abundance, Fertility, Creativity, Pleasure, Power, Feminine, Protection

Reversed Keywords

Tension, Insecurity, Infertility, Disharmony, Unproductive

The Emperor

The Number Four card of the Major Arcana. The Emperor represents a beneficial higher power and the presence of authority. He is the ultimate paternal figure and archetype of father. The Emperor expresses creative energy and the male qualities of assertiveness, troubleshooting, and taking directed action. He uses intermediaries and subordinates. While he maintains discipline, he lacks the passion held by the Empress. He enjoys setting and reaching concrete goals, and reflects action aimed at rational and organizational activities.

The Emperor is impartial and is rarely involved personally in situations. He is the pure expression of masculinity. He is known to be the part of us that creates habits and patterns and our learned behavior. He powers our decisions and judgements and is the part of us that orders the world. He is how we shape and form a potentially unruly existence.

The male counterpart of the Empress, he is a solid and stable man. Though he can be rigid and stubborn, he is a powerful protector. He signifies the dominance of logic and structure over our emotions. He has power and energy for life. The Emperor can indicate forgetting an important, spiritual part of yourself. He calls us to use our senses without the rational and logical parts of us completely dominating.

Upright

The Emperor reveals to us a powerful leader demanding our respect and authority. It means that as a leader you have a firm, but fair hand and a clear vision of what you want to create. You organize those around you to manifest goals and while you listen to their advice you have the final say. You are not afraid of conflict and you won't hesitate to protect those you care about by using your power. You are repaid with loyalty and the respect that you deserve. This card draws us to claim our authority as leaders and influencers, and to never let others put us down.

This card reflects the rules and regulations of a system. We can create law and order by applying guidelines to situations. By doing this we create calm out of chaos by breaking down a problem into its parts and creating the actions needed to resolve it. The Emperor tells us to take a strategic and organized approach and to stick to our plans until they are realized. He signifies expertise and worldly knowledge. Pulling this card can mean that you enjoy offering guidance and advice to those that may need it using the wisdom you have gained.

- o **Finance and career-** When you pull the Emperor upright, it may indicate an apex in your career, or the ability to become your own boss. It can represent your hard work finally paying off in terms of success and status. This could mean another person in your career that is willing to support you. The Emperor guides us to take logical and practical approaches to new job paths. Regarding finances, this card tells us to remain in control of our spending and to be aware of where our money is going.
- o **Love-** Could signify a romance with an older man or a powerful woman. It can represent a need to be more open with your feelings. Thought to mean a good sign for relationships, calling for stability and endurance in them.
- o **Health-** Can indicate being too hard on oneself, and a reminder to be gentle to our bodies and to work at our comfort levels. It's a call to seek medical treatment and to follow prescriptions but a good sign for health and for being well.

Reversed Reading

The Emperor reversed can signify being too rigid in your thinking. This can manifest as an abuse of authority, and over-use of power. This could be coming from you or another authoritative figure in your life and could even be coming from childhood issues with your father. This card reversed tells us to consider all the roles that power is currently playing in our lives. It begs us to ask ourselves if we are asserting our dominance and power in ways that leave others feeling powerless. It asks us to consider the ways we give away our personal power for the appeasement of others, especially those in authority. This can be a sign that others are looking to you as their expert and leader but that you are shying away from that role, preferring to stay out of the spotlight.

The reversed Emperor could be asking you to take a stand with an authority figure in your life. This could be a boss or an environment and when we see this card reversed, we need to pay attention to our self-discipline to get things done and our commitment to our goals. In relationships, a reversed card may suggest an unequal partnership. It brings attention to where our independence and freedoms may have been diminished by another's.

This could represent a sudden shock or a loss of control and temper. Reversed, the Emperor signifies relinquishing power and confusion regarding how to proceed forward. If not in relation to a person, it can represent your emotions and mind being out of balance. It begs that we stay logical and listen to our hearts to succeed.

Symbols for The Emperor- Illustration breakdown

- **Scepter**-A representation of the Emperors right to rule, and his reign. Typically represented by a globe and cross, the Scepter symbolizes the power he has over the material world.
- **Crown**- A symbol of strong will and dominance over emotions and instincts. Typically depicted with a long, white beard that represents his experience gained and the knowledge he has regarding ruling and being an authority over his people.
- **Throne**- The Emperor's throne signifies a concrete authority. This refers to stability and solidness. Adorned with the heads of Rams, his astrological sign of Aries is represented on the throne.
- **Ram's Heads-** The sign of Aries represents a strong will and the power of creation.
- **Mountains/Desert**- The Emperor is typically shown with barren mountains in the background. These can show his determination and ambition for greater heights. As opposed to the lush greenness found in the Empress card, these barren mountains represent a ruling with strength and force, and grit and highlight his leadership capability.

Keywords

Masculinity, Rigidity, Supremacy, Experience, Discipline, Domination, Rationalism, Tradition

Reversed Keywords

Stubbornness, Chaos, Loss of Control, Excessiveness, Submission

The Hierophant

The Number Five card. Along with the High Priestess and the Hermit, The Hierophant is one of the strongest spiritual cards in the Tarot. He is never wrong and works in complete harmony with the Universe. Acting as a bridge between spirits and men, and the sky and the earth.

The Hierophant is a traditionalist and calls us to value rules and laws. He represents the accepted forms and ways of teaching and knowledge. This card is connected to any spiritual notions we can come up with. It calls us to do the right thing and to remember that we must do the right thing for ourselves. Regarding spirituality and finding the right thing for ourselves, it calls us to stand up for our own beliefs. To create rules and systems to use in our lives to get us where we want to be.

While the High Priestess guards the mysteries, the Hierophant brings them to the people. He is a transmitter of wisdom, and counsel. He guards those dogmas of tradition and habits. He is the gateway to both material and spiritual knowledge and offers an objective point of view to help us learn. He asks that we do the same for others. His answers will appear in the form of questions.

Upright

The Hierophant reveals to us adherence to traditional ethics and rules. Fitting into society and being in the role of both student and mentor. When this card is drawn upright you may have concerns regarding your spirituality-and it calls you to make the time to allow your spirit to expand. He encourages us to learn those fundamental principles regarding our desires. This could mean working with a mentor or teacher about spiritual values and beliefs.

Also representing a wise authority figure the Hierophant signifies being part of a group or institution. If you do not have a sense of community, he calls us to identify with others and adopt ways of thinking to create further learning opportunities.

- **Finance and career**- When the Hierophant is pulled regarding money, it can represent avoiding risk or taking a route that is tested in ways to handle your money. This can mean seeking the advice of bankers and financial experts as it's a good time for investments in stable markets. He warns us against taking risks with our finances and spending too much. In your career, he signifies success if you are playing it by the rules.
- **Love**- Generally thought to be a good sign for those in relationships, the Hierophant represents commitment and having deep roots. It can also signify a new relationship that is built on love and commitment is on the way. He warns against going against conventional methods in obtaining and maintaining relationships.
- **Health**- This card calls us to bring healthy habits into our physical and mental lives. Rituals can be especially helpful for you right now. If there are challenges with health, it calls you to stick to conventional medicine as these traditional therapeutic means have a high chance of success now.

Reversed Reading

Upside down, the Hierophant reminds us that we are our own teachers. Seen as a guide for us to follow our own paths rather than others. This card reversed signifies a time where you are ready to go on your own and do things your own way-even if it's against convention. You no longer need external approval.

This card reversed also asks us to challenge the status quo. It says that we seek out opportunities to reclaim our personal powers and test the ideas that you were taught as the truth. He tells us that it is time to make our own rules. He also signifies a need to examine the way things are done and questioning their alignment with our values. This could represent a conflict with an authority figure as this card reversed can be interpreted as a rebellious teenager who questions society.

Pulling this card reversed can also mean that you are ignoring advice or have an unwillingness to learn. Be careful that you are not disrespecting your elders. The Hierophant reversed can represent a feeling of being restricted by structure and a loss of control and/or flexibility in your life.

Symbols for The Hierophant- Illustration breakdown

- **Columns**- The Hierophant sits between two pillars known to represent Rigor and Mercy. The columns are known as pillars in King Solomon's Temple.
- **3-Tiered Cross**- This triple scepter represents the three theological virtues Faith or Dogma, Hope or Prayer, and Charity or Benevolent Action. This scepter signifies his religious status.
- **3-Tiered Tiara**- Representing the three rules over which he rules; the conscious, subconscious, and superconscious. This signifies the ability to direct thought into those worlds at will.
- **Papal Coat**- Typically depicted wearing three robes one of red, blue, and white. This coat represents the Hierophants authority over spiritual matters.
- **Clerics**- At the feet of the Hierophant are found two followers, kneeling. This represents an initiation into the church or spiritual opportunities achieved through prayer and earnest request. This represents a rite of passage needed to enter the next level and having a shared group identity.
- **Naked Feet**- The Hierophant's naked feet signify his distance from material concerns as well as his humility.
- **Crossed Keys**- At his feet, these crossed keys show the ability to guide others and a balance between the conscious and subconscious minds. He holds the keys to wisdom and knowledge, and he can unlock those mysteries.

Keywords

Guidance, Religion, Wisdom, Ritual, Mentor, Instruction, Dogmatism, Spiritual Truth

Reversed Keywords

Unconventional, Rebel, Non-Conformity, Disillusionment, Rule Breaking

The Lovers

The Number Six card depicts free will and the human ability to choose. The Lovers represents a very strong emotional and sexual component and indicates romantic relationships. This can represent the union between lovers with vowed loyalty even when finding themselves exposed to dangers of jealousy and temptation.

Known for representing being in harmony with oneself, the Lovers is a card of raw honesty. We must be willing to be our most vulnerable in order to share our truest feelings.

The Lovers are the embodiment of the choices we make in life. They are the union of all opposites, and everything that we attract. This energy keeps humanity moving forward and is the wave of desire and attraction we feel. They advise us to choose wisely and feel everything as our desires and needs feed our creativity.

Upright

The Lovers reveals to us that by communicating honestly and openly with our loved ones we can create fulfilling and harmonious relationships that are built on respect and trust. When you pull this card, it can represent clarifying your beliefs and values. This could be a time where you are figuring out exactly what you stand for. You may be deciding what is essential to you. This card calls us to get out in the world and start making choices for ourselves while being true to ourselves.

Representing choice, the Lovers are a sign of a moral dilemma where we must consider all consequences before acting. This could be your values system is being challenged or that you are being called to take a higher path. They let us know that if we choose to love we choose the best version of ourselves.

The Lovers call us to unify dual forces, bringing together opposite parts to create something harmonious. They remind us that there is always an equal amount of positive and negative in a situation, as much challenge as there is an opportunity. They encourage us to accept this duality and build unity.

- **Finance and career-** The Lovers signify an attraction in money and finances. It may be a good time to seek new business opportunities or going for a new jo. Also representing a strong partnership of two people that work well together. It's also a reminder that business and love isn't always the best idea.
- **Love-** Known as a very positive for love, it can signify you are in or heading towards a lasting relationship that is worth committing yourself to. The bond and link between you will increase more than you could imagine, and it's a soulmate card. A good omen for the beginning of a relationship to those that are single.
- **Health-** The Lovers contain several meanings when representing the Health aspect of our lives. It can be a reassurance that you have the right support should any issues arise. It can indicate issues with any organs that are paired in our bodies such as kidneys, eyes, etc. The Lovers can also indicate choices that need to be made regarding treatment courses.

Reversed Reading

The Lovers reversed can signify a breakup of friends, relatives, and lovers. It can also mean that people are together for the wrong reasons. This can indicate a difficulty in making choices and a pattern of being in and out of relationships. When we see the Lovers upside down it lets us know of a wrong choice or one that was made from fear and haste.

This card can indicate an affair, or relationships that have gone sour or a break up. There may be a need to stabilize your emotions and end quarreling.

Symbols for The Lovers- Illustration breakdown

- **Angel-** An angel is shown above two nude figures and is thought to be Raphael which means "God heals." Raphael represents emotional and physical healing, as well as

blessings. His placement represents a sanctity of a higher power.
- **Snake/Tree of Knowledge**- Shown winding its way up the trunk of the fruit tree, the snake represents the nature of choice and the ramification of duality. The snake is a representation of the temptation of sensual pleasures and rebellion. The Tree of Knowledge represents gaining new knowledge and growth, and responsibility and awareness.
- **Nudity**- Signifying a complete vulnerability with the presence of each other the couple is at one with the nature around them. The man looks towards the woman, and the woman looks towards the angel-thought to represent a path from physical desire to spiritual concerns.
- **Tree of Life-**Shown behind the man, the Tree of Life is a symbol of ambition, and drive. The tree is shown with flames that represent passion and the nature and primary concern of man.
- **Mountain-** Sometimes depicted as volcanic, the mountain represents an eruption of passion when the two lovers meet. It's also showing the weight and reward of personal responsibility, and the solitude of choice.
- **Adam/Eve-** Eve signifies a receptive nature and the female, yin polarity while Adam signifies a creative nature and the male, yang polarity

Keywords

Love, Choice, Harmony, Passion, Eros, Bonding, Affection, Pleasure

Reversed Keywords

Conflict, Disagreement, Opposition, Disharmony, Confusion, Pressure

The Chariot

The Seventh Card of the Major Arcana. The Chariot represents our will-power and determination. One who is reaching and enjoying their success due to their own labor and ingenuity. This card indicates a sense of forward motion and the need to take the reins of a situation. This is a person who knows what they want and how they will get it.

The Chariot shows that Strength will overcome all obstacles in our way. He is the essence of realizing what we want and going for it. His strength is in acting, movement, and the motions that power us to where we want to be. When we take action in our lives he will be at the wheel. As we steer our course, he provides us energy.

If we maintain our focus, determination, and confidence we will be able to get through the challenges and detours we find on our journey. The Chariot reminds us that aggression is part of our nature and that it can be used in taking charge of situations but that we must rein it in from hindering the way forward.

Upright

When the Chariot is interpreted, it is a sign of encouragement. Your inner power and dedication will bring your objectives to you. The Chariot calls us to use our willpower, and discipline and commitment to achieve our goals. It means taking an active role in making things work out for yourself and sticking to the course no matter what challenges we may face.

The Chariot is seen as a sign of success and a call to be courageous. He tells us to be bold and have faith in ourselves and what we stand for. He begs us to have faith in ourselves and to lay down our boundaries with others. Literally, it can represent taking a trip, especially driving.

- **Finance and career**- The Chariot urges us to push through and tells us that we will succeed. This represents being motivated and ambitious. You have a high chance of winning competitions, and this is great news for your money. He can represent a business trip and coming into extra money.
- **Love**- When you draw the Chariot regarding love it can show competitiveness in the relationship. It can also

point us to loving ourselves first and foremost-and that our current relationship status is a reflection of how well we do that. The Chariot asks us to balance our minds and emotions to be successful and points out that hard work and focus are needed to resolve issues. If Single, the card shows there may still be pain from your past but that it can be overcome by moving forward.
- **Health-** A good sign for health, the Chariot shows that we are on the path to a full recovery from any issues. It can also point to health issues within the digestive system that needs to be resolved.

Reversed Reading

This can represent a lack of willpower or becoming aware of one's aggressions. While it can signify an unhealthy obsession with goals it can also direct you to a lack of direction, or motivation. In reverse, the Chariot asks that we come to terms with not always being in control. He asks us to come up with the courage to emerge victoriously.

The Chariot in reverse is giving up before you really got started, maybe because of being self-conscious. He begs you to take your control back and stop being a passenger. This can also indicate issues with your vehicle. This card may be a hint that by attempting to manage every little detail in our lives we lose more control. We must learn to let things run their course and loosen the reins.

Symbols for The Chariot- Illustration breakdown

- **Curtains-** Adorned with celestial symbols showing a connection to the Divine Will. This heavenly canopy protects and monitors the driver.
- **Crown-** Typically shown with a laurel and star crown that signals spiritual evolution, success, and victory. The crown shows the nobility of spiritual dignity.
- **Armor-** The Chariot's armor is shown with crescent moons that are meant to represent what is coming into being. The alchemical symbols that the armor is adorned with represent spiritual transformation and show the power of the Chariot came from conquest and strength.

- **Winged Solar Disc/Shield-** Symbolizing the inner drive and the balance of both the yin and yang nature.
- **Sphinxes-** Both sphinxes are under the control of the Charioteer, but they are driving him forward into the unknown as they pull in opposite directions. The Charioteer uses sheer resolve to steer in the direction he wants. They represent the two opposing natures of direction and choice. One sphinx is black, and one is white signaling the duality in nature, the positive and the negative.
- **Walled City/River-** The Chariot can sometimes be shown in front of a city that indicates his domain and power is limited to the realm of man. The River is symbolic of needing to flow with the current of the rhythm of life and to also charge forward towards your intentions.

Keywords

Progress, Energy, Ambition, Progress, Action, Command, Confidence

Reversed Keywords

Defeat, Powerlessness, Cowardice, Aggression, Obstacles

Strength

The Eighth card of the Major Arcana, Strength speaks to our inner strength and the ability of the human spirit to overcome all obstacles. This is about knowing that you can endure the obstacles in life. Strength reflects calmness trumping brutality, and order reigns over chaos.

Strength symbolizes a conflict between oppositional motivations and desires. For new possibilities to emerge, one must be defeated. She also represents the knowing of how to overcome obstacles without violence. She shows a great persistence that we have, and to go about things in a way that shows our maturity and composure.

The Strength card represents the growing connection you have to your inner self. She is a reminder that even in hard times you have the power to turn things your way. This can represent a very spiritual time even in the absence of organized religion or beliefs. Using finesse and soft touch you can get what you want with the ability to channel this great power. Representing a softness, Strength is our higher softness over carnal desires.

Upright

Strength shows us that we are fueled by inner-strength and determination. Instead of trying to control others you persuade and influence to achieve your goals. Because this power is mostly unseen, you can be underestimated by others. This is an advantage to you as you can control situations without outward or excessive force. She shows us that sometimes no one knows that you are the one calling the shots.

Strength is the reserves of your power needed to get things done and to forge our way in the world. She tells us that we have only just scratched the surface of our abilities and she gives us the confidence to overcome any doubts. She begs that even when we feel the fear that we do it anyway. Pulling the Strength card shows that you are a loyal supporter and friend that is willing to step up and be present when it's needed. You may be compelled to hold space for someone who needs that support and strength you possess.

This card begs we channel our initial responses of raw emotion into constructive feelings and actions. What you do with your emotions is what makes all the difference in a situation. When we approach situations from a place of compassion and love we bring our urges into balance with the greater good.

- **Finance and career**- The Strength card is a positive symbol for promotion and raises in pay. If you're looking career-wise, she urges you to keep pushing as you have everything you need to get what you want. When it comes to finances this could be a sign of stability with your money, and that well thought out investments and large purchases will move forward the way you want them to.
- **Love-** When you see the Strength card regarding love it can be a sign that the relationship, you're in is stable and that there is plenty of room for you both to grow. It can

also mean it's time to go for new love as your confidence rules. She also represents meeting someone that may have a wild side.
- o **Health-** A good sign for health-related queries. This shows health is improving or is good.

Reversed Reading

The Strength card in reverse calls us to take stock of our energy levels and encourages us to withdraw for a bit. This tells us we must take care of ourselves if we are to take care of others. She tells us that we have more resilience and strength than we know and that we can re-energize our self-assurance by looking at your past.

Tune into your inner strength and confidence to measure where they stand and how they are acting in our lives. She begs us to ask what we can do to bring these things back into balance. When reversed, Strength also can point to explosive behaviors and being aggressive. She warns that you do not do something that you may come to regret. She urges you to learn to channel your emotions so that they do not harm you or others. She calls us to speak with others to deal with emotions and loss of control.

Symbols for Strength- Illustration breakdown

- **Infinity/Lemniscate-** This speaks of the quiet fortitude that comes from the union of physical and moral strength. This shows Strength's infinite potential and wisdom.
- **Hands-** Her hands are holding or stroking the jaws of a lion indicating the ability to control anger and rage. Strength's hands reflect a soft touch that is both humble and assertive through their gentle movement. This shows the beast was tamed with loving, calm energy.
- **Maiden-** Depicted with a white robe, or being plain-clothed, this reflects her purity of spirit. The Maiden signifies the strength of reason as well as having both a moral and righteous strength.
- **Lion-** Known as a symbol of raw passion, physical strength, and desire. The Lion is taught by Strength that these things can be expressed positively when resilience and inner strength are applied.

- **Walled Castle-** Sometimes shown with a castle in the distance representing how true strength is found to exist outside of the common manifestations of power.

Keywords

Power, Fortitude, Strength, Composure, Energy, Patience, Force

Reversed Keywords

Fear, Weakness, Vulnerability, Obstacles

The Hermit

The Ninth Card of the Major Arcana, the Hermit represents Spiritual Journey. The Hermit is completely focused on the substance of things and contemplates peace. He is regarded as a Master and is looked to with respect. His self-imposed solitude is an element of his research as he moves away from the noise of the world for deep introspection.

The Hermit strives to understand and internalize what is brought before him. He is the place where you examine and cultivate your spiritual truth. He is the renewal of self through observation and reflection.

Solitude and Withdrawal are what the Hermit urges us to seek. If we have had a hard time we should focus on our own needs and even seek out someone wise to help guide us. We must remove ourselves from a situation to see the answers inside of ourselves.

Upright

The Hermit signifies a time to contemplate motivations, principles, and personal values in an effort to know your authentic self on a deeper level. He shows a break from everyday life and focusing attention inward to realize your most profound truths.

Appearing during those times when you are considering new directions in your life. The Hermit urges us to meditate and re-evaluate our personal goals so that we can take the correct course. This can also mean turning away from a materialistic existence to focus on your inner world. The Hermit shows us that the answers we seek are within and that we can discover them through quiet and solitude.

A Spiritual mentor in your life, the Hermit represents this person being able to enhance your consciousness and raise your vibration. This person can teach you how to find your own answers.

- o **Finance and career-** When the Hermit appears regarding money it can show excessive focus in that area of your life. It can mean you have questions regarding the right career path. This is not a time for risky investments, but it can indicate a desire to invest in professional development.
- o **Love-** Be honest with yourself. The Hermit guides us to ask ourselves if we know who we really are, and what we really want. Regarding Love, the Hermit can show a period of solitude or a need to recover and heal from something in the past. He asks that we give ourselves time to rest and start again renewed.
- o **Health-** The Hermit asks that you do not push yourself too hard as it may lead to health problems. He urges us to reduce the stress in our lives by putting our needs first. Meditative practice and plenty of rest are crucial for our health.

Reversed Reading

The Hermit reversed represents taking too much time for personal reflection, or not enough. If you are not spending enough time on this personal reflection, the Hermit urges you to create more space to reflect and go deeper into your inner being. He guides us to focus on rebuilding ourselves on a spiritual level and rediscover our greater purpose on Earth.

If you are spending time on this inner reflection you may be taking the isolation too far. The reversed Hermit begs us to value our connection to others, even on this spiritual journey. He guides us to make time for loved ones and to not become too absorbed in personal dilemmas. Reversed, He can also signify unwelcome isolation from someone in your life. Find the balance in relationships and explore reconnections.

The reverse Hermit may indicate exhaustive socializing or having excess need of others in your life. Do not allow any sense of loneliness or isolation to hold you back.

Symbols for The Hermit- Illustration breakdown

- **Beard-** The Hermit's beard is a sign of age and wisdom. A renunciation of vanity in all forms.
- **Hood-** Giving up a connection to identity and representing the ability to maintain secret thoughts.
- **Cloak-** The Hermit's cloak shows his humility and a focus on inwardness as opposed to outward appearance.
- **Sandals-** Thought to represent the sacrifices that may be needed to seek enlightenment. The Hermit's sandals express the hardship of the road.
- **Staff-** This shows the Hermit's willingness to lead others.
- **Lantern-** Typically shown in the Hermit's right hand, his lantern has a six-pointed star on the inside, the Seal of Solomon. Being a symbol of wisdom, it represents the inner light illuminating the road ahead. This also signifies a continuous quest for enlightenment.
- **Desert-** Indicating solitude and as the Hermit stands on the top of a mountain, it shows spiritual mastery and accomplishment. This is the path he has chosen, and he has reached a heightened state of awareness regarding self-discovery.

Keywords

Wisdom, Silence, Pilgrimage, Observation, Austerity, Retreat

Reversed Keywords

Withdrawal, Isolation, Concealment, Loneliness

The Wheel of Fortune

The Tenth Card in the Major Arcana. When we come across the Wheel of Fortune, we move from personality types of the Major Arcana into experiential forces. The Wheel is always turning, and we must understand changes are imminent. The card urges us to cherish the good and to make the most of them while we have them in front of us because they can be gone just as quickly as they came in.

The Wheel of Fortune calls us to be kind and loving to others so that they will treat us the same way. This card reminds us that what we are sending out into the Universe is returned to us so we must focus on abundance and positive energy in this regard. Provide the Universe with faith and optimism so that it will take care of your situation in the best way.

Open yourself to the help of others. This includes synchronicities and signs from the Universe that support us along our journeys. The Physical and Spiritual realms want us to do well and we should call on them anytime we need. The Wheel is also a reminder to accept what we are dealing with and adapt.

When you see the Wheel of Fortune it can signify a turning point in your life. This can be positive opportunities that are unexpected and unfamiliar. The Wheel gives us an invitation to take a new direction in life and asks that we let our intuition to guide us.

Upright

A sign of success and good luck, the Wheel of Fortune urges us to not miss our chance for what we want. This is a chance that is given to us and we must use our intention and focus to use it. Also, a symbol of cycles and karma, we must remember this when we are experiencing troubled times.

The Wheel of Fortune is more material than spiritual and with fate on our side, we can develop ourselves spiritually. Use any guidance or assistance we meet wisely as it's up to use to interpret signs and understand them. This card symbolizes the flow of time and the nature of life. The Wheel calls us to maintain equilibrium as we will ride high and low repeatedly.

Pulling this card may mean the beginning of a new cycle in your life. Thought to represent a change of luck for the better, the Wheel reminds us that nothing lasts forever.

- o **Finance and career**- The Wheel of Fortune shows us that changes are coming. It's a good time to go for the things you want in your career and that you may expect a promotion or raise. A new position may be coming to

you and your finances will improve. Regarding gambling, you may be lucky, but the card urges us to remember that fates change from moment to moment.
- o **Love-** Generally a good sign regarding relationships. Good changes are on the way and you have time to make your relationships better. This could also mean that it's time to end a relationship as now is a good time for splitting away. This card shows us that no matter what you will be lea to where you are meant to be. A card for those lucky in love.
- o **Health-** Changes for the better may be headed your way. This could be an improvement in health issues you've been experiencing. The Wheel of Fortune urges us to make lifestyle changes that will improve our health. This can be rest, or just taking better care of ourselves.

Reversed Reading

The Wheel of Fortune reversed signifies a change for the worse. This could be obstacles in your future or failing in the future. This is a calling for preparedness. Being cyclical in nature, the Wheel of Fortune shows us that even in hard times we know our fates will turn back to good.

Symbols for The Wheel of Fortune- Illustration breakdown

- **Sphinx-** Sitting on top of the wheel, the Sphinx symbolizes perpetual change and the fateful forces of the unconscious. The Sphinx represents strength and knowledge.
- **Anubis-** Known as the Egyptian God of the dead, Anubis welcomes souls to the underworld. Rising on the outer circle heading upwards. Known as a symbol of death and/or fate.
- **Snake-** On the outer circle facing downwards, it represents the life force as it plunges into the material world. Known to represent the God Typhon, the God of Evil and the deadliest in mythology.
- **Tetramorph-** The four-winged creatures found in the corners of the card. Representing the four fixed signs of the zodiac and guardians of the four directions of space. They are defenders against a return to chaos. The Angel

represents Aquarius, The Eagle represents Scorpio, The Lion represents Leo, and The Bull represents Taurus. Their wings show stability through change. Each figure is holding the Torah, representing their wisdom.

- **Wheel and Symbology-** The wheel itself indicates the cyclic nature of fortune and fate.
  - On the middle wheel, the alchemical symbols for Mercury, Sulphur, Water, and Salt are shown representing the building blocks of life. This is also the representation of the four elements, signifying formative power.
  - T.A.R.O.- Thought to mean ROTA, or "wheel" in Latin, these letters also arrange to Tora meaning "law, and Tarot.
  - Hebrew Letters YHVH (the unpronounceable name of God). The Tetragrammaton Yod, Heh, Vau, Heh

Keywords

Revolution, Repetition, Fate, Expansion, Possibilities, Change

Reversed Keywords

Negative, Downturn, Bad Luck

Justice

Card number eleven. The embodiment of the search for balance in all conflicting forces, Justice represents fairness and truth. The Justice card shows us that morals do not only depend on one's opinion but that they come from a greater, karmic source. Her scales show the balance of opposites. This can represent the heart versus the head, spirit versus matter, and unconsciousness versus consciousness. Her scales show the ability to ascertain and understand right from wrong.

Justice's sword symbolizes being able to act and being able to separate unjust and just actions. When we see Justice, we may be called to account for our actions, and be judged. If we are in alignment with our Higher Selves and act for the greater good of others we need not worry. Otherwise, expect to be called out and be prepared to own up to your actions. This isn't a black and white judgement as there is a certain compassion and understanding that Justice brings with her.

The Justice card symbolizes a search for the truth. She calls us to prepare to explore what that truth means to us. Challenge yourself and explore your belief system to create awareness around what you believe to be true as well as what you believe to be ethical and fair.

Upright

Justice may appear when an important decision needs to be made. She asks us how the impact of this decision will affect or impact others well-being as well as ourselves. Be prepared to stand by the decision you make as you will be held accountable for them. Use your inner guidance and intuition to find the decision that is in alignment with the highest good.

If you are seeking justice in your life, this card indicates that it will be served. Justice reminds us that we must accept and move on from any decisions that are made as there are no second chances in this regard. Justice reminds us that we will get what we give. We must consider others when making judgements and choices. Justice reveals the answers we seek and represents our effort, our moral center, and our life's work.

Justice always reminds us to keep an open mind and to always be fair in situations. This means always doing the right thing even in the face of difficult challenges. She represents a restoration of balance and sowing seeds for the future.

- o **Finance and career**- Justice represents doing things the right way. She shows us that it's better to correct mistakes that come to light rather than concealing them. Also referring to the balance between personal life and career. When Justice is pulled regarding money, she represents clarity and being rewarded for treating finances with respect and fairness.
- o **Love-** In relationships Justice shows that your partner will treat you like you treat them. This can mean the truth coming out about secrets and a call for balancing your relationships. A good omen to find a new love and a reference to virginity and purity. Can signify someone with the astrological sign of Libra entering your life, or someone in the legal field.

- **Health-** Justice shows us to balance our lifestyle. Do not push too hard with diet and exercise just as you do not need to be excessively lazy. Moderation and balance are key to our well-being.

Reversed Reading

When you see the Justice card reversed it can point to something you've done that isn't morally right. Though others might not be aware you have to make the choice to hide it or own up to it so that you can resolve the situation. You will live with the consequences, either way, so you must do what feels right to you.

She can also represent an unwillingness to take accountability for your actions or blaming others for your mistakes. Justice asks us to assess our situations again and discover where we can accept responsibility. Once you do what you can to make things right again you free yourself from guilt and raise your personal power regarding making decisions.

Reversed, Justice shows us that your inner critic is active. She reminds us to start from a place of self-acceptance and forgiveness, compassion and kindness. She urges us to give thanks to the inner critic and then clear it away. When making important decisions, Justice shows that we may need more information before a balanced decision can be made.

Symbols for Justice- Illustration breakdown

- **Crown-** A sign of illuminated existence and clarified ideas. Shown with a small square on the crown, this represents well-ordered thoughts and symbolizes sunlight.
- **Columns-** Indicating a sacred temple showing us law, structure, and balance.
- **Sword-** In Justice's right hand, the sword shows her logical mindset needed for fair justice. Her sword symbolizes logic, rationality, and impartial judgement. Pointing upwards, the sword expresses a final decision while the double-edged blade shows the consequences of all actions.
- **Scales-** In her left hand known to symbolize intuition, Justice holds scales that show intuition must balance logic.

- Her scales represent a careful balancing, impartiality, and attentive care.
- **Veil-** Justice sits in front of a veil that represents the hidden ways and reasons of Justice. This refers to the hidden knowledge that controls the sometimes-mysterious ways of Justice.

Keywords

Logic, Balance, Judging, Equality, Fairness, Legalism

Reversed Keywords

Injustice, Dishonesty, Corruption, Bigotry

The Hanged Man

The twelfth card of the deck. Generally, the Hanged Man card represents a certain lack of ability when it comes to helping yourself by your own means. It can be interpreted as literally a man hanging, unable to regain control of any situation until it has passed or awaiting judgement. This card calls for a time of inward focus and meditation regarding the position you are in. This introspection should be turned into action once you are free again. The Hanged Man begs us to grasp the lesson in the experience and to understand that only those with the patience and wisdom can see through these limitations.

Remember that discomfort and even suffering are necessary for personal growth and evolution. The Hanged Man can represent a moment of being unable to act, or of difficulty. It seems that he has offered himself up for this test voluntarily. The symbolism of the Hanged Man being upside down representing initiation rituals indicates a transition from one level of consciousness to another. Hanging between two separate levels of awareness he is a symbol of changing perspectives and understanding other points of view. When you approach the world with fresh eyes and a new point of view, the energy of the Hanged Man awakens. When we sacrifice ourselves and push past through the uncomfortable limits, we see that we don't remain there for too long.

It's the realization of what may be hidden to us otherwise by taking a pause to contemplate new perspectives. We can do this ourselves when it's needed as the Universe will do it for us if we do not. The Hanged Man asks that we use our intuition to develop a sense of when the time is right to take that pause, before things get out of hand. We need to surrender ourselves to the opportunity of reflection, even when that comes with unexpected and abrupt halts to the activities in our lives. We must understand that there is something new emerging that we will not see until enough space and time has been allowed for it to reveal itself. When we resist, we find more obstacles driving us to where we are meant to be.

Upright

The Hanged Man advises us to give up our illusions of control and accept the fact that we need to lie in the beds we've made. This is not necessarily negative but perhaps inconvenient or even embarrassing in some cases. Contemplate how you have collaborated with the problem that has led you to this point of required pause. Remember the time that you spend here is not wasted and eventually, you will be grateful for being derailed from the path you were on. He reminds us that refraining from action can bring the same or more benefits as acting with urgency.

When this card appears in a reading it can indicate a feeling of shame, of being a victim or feeling trapped. While it is useless to fight against it, the Hanged Man begs that you take lessons from it to become a better person. He also indicates that you have decisions to make but that things are going against the way you had hoped or planned. He begs that we release negative thoughts and old ways of thinking and beliefs so that we can allow this new path to develop before us. When you see the Hanged Man, think of it as a crossroads that signifies it's possible to clear the slate and begin again.

- **Finance and career-** Don't rush into any decisions regarding your career path where you might feel stuck or uncertain. Learn to tell the difference between that is important and what is urgent to you. This indicates you should take a new perspective on your finances and learn the basics of handling them. This isn't necessarily negative but a call to look at your financial situation

another way. The Hanged Man can indicate a time to share your blessings, however limited. It can signify you have in your life someone that will not hesitate to share their blessings with you.
- o **Love-** When you pull the Hanged Man regarding Love, it can indicate unhappiness in current relationships. It's time to focus on what's important for both of you. If you are unhappy, the Hanged Man reminds us that we keep ourselves in the situation. When single it can indicate a need to do something different, even opposite of what you're currently doing. He calls in a multitude of options for you but warns against wasting an opportunity with indecision. In general, the card is calling you to let go. Let go of those bad experiences, thoughts, decisions, lovers, and let the good come in and have space in your life.
- o **Health-** The Hanged Man is urging you to explore all options available to you. You can achieve the results you want by looking at different angles. Because the card signifies being stuck in a situation that you feel that you just can't get out of, it can indicate a feeling of frustration in trying to overcome an illness. A positive sign when dealing with health issues, this card begs you to consider all solutions

Reversed Reading

Reversed, the Hanging Man can recall a time where you feel that you're not getting anything in return for the period you are sacrificing. It can represent a time of no resolution, or a standstill with no movement. This can feel like nothing turns out the way it should even though you are dedicating all your energy and effort into making it so. When you have already taken the time out when you pull this card, it could suggest that it's time to move forward with your new perspective and renewed energy. Regarding relationships, the Reversed Hanged Man points to a realization that you should not rush things but that there comes a time when you must decide.

The Hanged Man when in reverse can indicate a reluctance to act or decide something. He advises us not to wait until you feel all the way ready since that will probably never happen. He advises that we take the leap ourselves before the Universe doesn't wait for us. This can indicate certain behaviors that aren't suiting you any longer, your attitudes, and things that have happened. When you see this card reversed it can mean that this difficult period is coming to an end and that there is no going back. We determine our own futures with those attitudes we have about our lives.

Symbols for The Hanged Man- Illustration breakdown

- **Hanging Beam-** This can symbolize a boundary between the two states of existence, or even opinions. The Beam symbolizes a crossroads and choices to be made.
- **Crossed legs-** An act symbolic of martyrdom, his bent and folded leg show that this may be voluntary. The arms behind his back symbolize powerlessness.
- **Tree -** thought to be the Living World Tree, it's rooted deep in the underworld and supports the heavens. Trees symbolize knowledge and life.
- **Upside down Hanging-** The Hanged Man being hung from his foot upside down indicates a complete reversal in point of view. Literally seeing the world from a different perspective.
- **Halo-** Through perseverance and suffering come wisdom and enlightenment. Symbolic of intellect and power.

Keywords

Martyrdom, Release, Surrendering, Limbo, Inversion, Contemplation

Reversed Keywords

Stalling, Impulsiveness, betrayal, Apathy, Detachment

The Death Card

The thirteenth card of the Major Arcana. Carrying elements of unexpected change and suddenness, the Death card refers to letting go of the past and starting over. There is no need to fear this card as figuratively Death can call to end many things in our lives and mark the beginning of new things. In any case, the Death card destroys our sense of security and forces us to venture beyond. This ending can cause us grief and this disruption can bring about positive change. The Death card indicates a loss or ending of certain relationships and connections with people and things.

This card tells us to cut the ties between the past and future regarding certain people, or situations. This is also a card of acceptance. Understand that everyone dies, and no one evades Death. Understand also that we lose friends, we end relationships, and we lose jobs in a constant cycle that never ends for anyone. We must bring our focus on what we stand to gain. Death is a very positive card especially if you are in the process of letting go of something or entering new territory. This includes spiritual transformations as well as behavioral and habitual. We need not worry over the threat of physical death. The Death card can signal that you are ready for certain changes to take place in your life.

Almost always indicating the end of an impactful relationship it can be accompanied by regret and anger, but it will also be followed by relief and comfort. The Death card reminds us to give ourselves the space we need to grieve and come to terms with feelings of loss. You will begin to understand yourself on a deeper level when you can appreciate those things you still have even during experiences of loss and endings. The Death card advises that if you are in a dark place, a brighter, colorful place is being manifested or realized at the same time. Welcome to the paradigm shift.

Upright

The Death card signifies an end to a major phase in your life and marks the beginning of a new phase. It's up to you to close the door you are exiting through as it must be shut before the other, new door opens. The Death card calls us to focus our energies on what lies ahead. Seeing this card in a spread can indicate a time of transition where the old version must die for the new one to be created. The Death card urges us to welcome this change and the life events it will bring to us. Keep moving forward and let go of any unhealthy attachments.

This card can appear when you feel swept up in change that you can't control or feeling caught in an upheaval. The Death card advises we let go of old ways of life and to move forward, away from them. If you are breaking habits and certain patterns of behavior, this is a great card to see. Now is the time to let go of excess and those unnecessary things in your life by purging out the old things that get in the way.

- **Finance and career-** This card advises that sacrifices should be made in facing our financial situation. There could be a coming loss in income or a change in your responsibilities. It is also a call to remove the unnecessary from our lives and to go back and reevaluate what's truly important. Big changes are coming.
- **Love-** If the Death card is pulled regarding Love it can a sign to let go of a relationship you have been trying to save. Only through introspection and communication will you know if it's the right time to let things end.
- **Health-** If you find the Death card in a spread regarding Health-related matters don't fret. This is a sign that long term issues can and will resolve themselves in positive and natural ways. Death advises us to embrace these changes and focus on how we are living.

Reversed Reading

The Death card reversed can represent a resistance you have to change that must be dealt with. Even in reverse, the Death card urges us to let go of what is past or what is so that things can work in our favor. This card reversed advises that we take a realistic view and let go of anything that is no longer serving us. It can be difficult, but once you've gone through this transformation new energy will come into your life.

Symbols for Death- Illustration breakdown

- **Armored Skeleton-** An embodiment of Death, or messenger. This is the part of our bodies that survive after life has gone. The armor signifies the invincibility of Death, and the black color indicates mystery and mourning while the horse is white - the color of purity, strength, and power.

- **Black Banner with Mystic Rose-** Symbolizing life, beauty, immortality, and change. Life and Death are connected, and there is beauty in both.
- **Fallen King-** indicating that Death spares no one and that everything in our Material world is fated to pass. Everyone is alike before Death. The crown is shown knocked off the King's head and laying on the ground indicating that the old ways are now overthrown.
- **Bishop/Woman/Child-** seemingly pleading and praying in the presence of Death, the Bishop seems to be surrendering. The woman and child beg to be spared.
- **Boat on River-**Representing boats that escort the dead to the afterlife, and the fact that Life will continue onward regardless of change.
- **Sun/Towers-** In the background on the horizon the sun is setting between two towers signifying immortality, hope, and how even with the death of flesh there is the birth of spirit. This symbolizes a sense of dying every night and being reborn every morning.

Keywords

Transformation, Elimination, Cleansing, Radical, Fatality, Expiration, Threshold

Reversed Keywords

Stagnation, Sleep, Inertia, Dependency, Resistance, Fighting being uprooted

Temperance

The fourteenth card of the Major Arcana, Temperance, brings the energy of peace, and patience. A card that signifies the right balance between spiritual and material things. Temperance is a card indicative of finding a sense of inner peace and calm and having a good perspective. Temperance has harmonious relationships with others and self. This card advises us to listen to our inner guidance because our spirit guides are surrounding us. Remain patient with the path you are on and the pace it is moving forward, as it is developing exactly how it should.

The Temperance card of the Major Arcana asks us to stabilize our energies and recover our own flow in life to achieve and maintain order and balance. In the same way that we "temper" an object or material so can we refine out skills and talents to become more diligent. It's the holding of opposites objectively so that a third option appears, and a true path emerges. Re-examine the priorities you've chosen and evaluated where you will benefit from more balance in your life. Temperance carries a suggestion that excess or extremes of any situation should be avoided.

Upright

The Temperance card indicates that you experience peace and tranquility and that you are in touch with your inner self. It can represent energy that does not allow issues and conflicts to disrupt its balance. This card calls us to pursue our spiritual paths with patience. This is a card of higher learning. You may be experiencing a time of learning many things and having a sense of peace while you do so. It's a good indicator of someone listening and following their own inner voice.

Temperance symbolizes blending and mixing different elements to create something new and more valuable than any of the parts individually. This is accompanied by a sense of confidence and having a long-term vision of what you want to achieve, and the time it will take for you to reach that point. Temperance calls us to be peacekeepers and to bring others together in the spirit of cooperation and harmony. This card's energy is calm even in the face of stress. It's an even temperament and effectively managing emotions.

- **Finance and career-** Temperance signifies a good time to set goals as you are likely to achieve what you want through dedication and hard work. The card speaks to patience and moderation.
- **Love-** One of the best cards to pull for relationships, the Temperance card can indicate soulmates. It can represent resolved issues and finding a perfect balance with your love. It can also bring that balance into all areas of our lives in order to make more room for a loving partner.

- **Health-** The upright Temperance indicates a need for balance in areas that need healing. Get unhealthy habits under control, reevaluate what you are spending energy on.

Reversed Reading

When Temperance is reversed there may be an overindulgent behavior or an imbalance in your life. It can indicate being hasty or behaving recklessly. This card shows an excess of indulgence and a loss with our inner calm. This can be disharmony with people in our lives or being pulled into the drama of others. Temperance reversed can show a lack of looking at the big picture when it comes to your behavior. The card advises that we evaluate the root causes so that we can work to resolve them. In situations involving love, this card can denote a strong imbalance and the need to find one's inner balance before having success with harmonious relationships.

You may be experiencing a type of spiritual imbalance where you feel disconnected from your guides and intuition. It can be a disconnection inside of yourself, where meditative practices can help bring you back to your center. Take note of anything that feels "off" in your life or anything that is causing you tension and stress. Make the adjustments needed to get back into your balanced flow. Temperance guides us to focus on the long-term vision for our life and our higher purpose so that we can align our day to day activities to these things. Reversed, Temperance indicates a period of self-evaluation where we may run into conflict while creating the needed balance and healing.

Symbols for Temperance- Illustration breakdown

- **Wings-** The wings of the angel signifies the intention of the Universe and benevolent healing. The angel also shows a sun just above their forehead. This indicates the power of transmutation.
- **Path-** off to the side is a path that symbolizes our journey between rational understanding, and spiritual understanding.

- **Sun/Mountain-** The sun rising over the mountain indicates an ascension to the spiritual realm and being freed from the limits of the intellectual world.
- **Water-** Symbolic of Life, and purification. The angel has one foot on the earth representing the material world, and one foot in the water represents the subconscious. This symbolizes an ability to balance both material and psychic energies.
- **Blending-** Temperance is shown blending the water into two different cups. This represents union and the infinite nature of the super and subconscious minds being blended. This is representative of a gentle change and the removal of excess.

Keywords

Meekness, Harmony, Moderation, Recovery, Healing, Synergy

Reversed Keywords

Religion, Recklessness, Excess, Discord

The Devil

The Devil card, the fifteenth in the Major Arcana, comes with a lot of negative connotations. In the Fool's Journey, when he encounters the Devil, he is told that the beast simply brings out what is already inside of him. The Devil assures him that there is nothing to fear or avoid and that these desires and temptations of the material world can help in the quest to spirituality. The figures in the card seem to be chained up in a visual representation of "as you reap so shall you sow" but they can take their collars off if they wish. The Devil card shows that there are some of us that will want to remain controlled by our bestial, primal desires and those of us that understand them for what they are and allow them in moderation as a tool of power.

This Tarot Card depicts the god of nature and of wild behavior, not actually Satan. One way to interpret the Devil card is to understand the need to be honest with ourselves. It's a call to ask ourselves if we are holding ourselves back from what we desire and what we take pleasure in. It begs us to ask what we are allowed to have power over us, and what makes us feel powerful so that we can reach our highest goals. The Devil card can represent a person in your life that is powerful, and hard to resist. It warns against allowing this person to provide you a sense of identity. It can also represent ourselves. Are we encouraging others to act the way we want? This can form our identities as well and create codependent relationships.

Ask yourself if there is anything you find hard to resist? The Devil card shows us that when we recognize those things in our life that keep us held captive, we have the power to change it. There is no need to fear the Devil card. As with any other card, it helps us understand a part of ourselves so that we can gain control over it and use that power for the greater good.

Upright

When the Devil card is pulled, it can show that we have feelings of emptiness or a lack of contentment in our lives. This card is associated with indulgence and can signify being materialistic and not being able to turn down luxuries. This card symbolizes temptation and warns that though it may feel good to us we become trapped in our own obsessions and addictions. The Devil warns that we do not give up control of ourselves and our destinies. This card is about illusions and how we can create them to continue our behavior. This card guides us to identify the devils in our own lives. What are we slaves to? What are those things in our lives that can lead to this obsessive behavior that we can rectify now?

Not always a negative interpretation, the Devil card can also reflect the need to lose control and start enjoying the pleasures in this material existence. The Devil reminds us to do so without excess and without fear. This card usually refers to feeling trapped and not having our own choice in the matter. Take the time to see how this card relates to the others in a spread as they can help you interpret where changes need to be made or areas in your life that need extra focus.

The Devil card in the upright position can point to something in your life that you may not realize is holding you back. This is a warning that you take care of these things now, while you are still able. Regarding the future, the Devil card implies that something will not end well if you do not make serious changes now.

- o **Finance and career**- Pulling the Devil card regarding personal finance can indicate a realignment of priorities is needed. It can also refer to someone in your life that is playing against you and begs that you think carefully about those you trust. It can be an indication that you are spending too much money on those things you do not need and warns that we take time to handle our finances wisely. The Devil card also points to someone in your career that you should not trust. This may be someone that shows an easy road to success or offering positions that seem too good.
- o **Love-** The Devil card urges us to explore desires and experiences without shame, and with full acceptance that it's okay to enjoy ourselves in consenting relationships. On the flip side, the Devil card can show jealously or envy in a partnership and even cheating or sexual assault. When single, this card can refer to having sex without love. While that is perfectly okay, it's wise to remember the consequences of the actions we take.
- o **Health-** If you are participating in destructive behavior, you may see the Devil card in relation to health matters. This card reminds us that we need to ask for help when we need it, and to not feel shame over what we've done up to this point. It's a call to re-evaluate our habits and break free from them. The Devil card urges us to check in on our health even when we are in good health.

Reversed Reading

When the Devil card is pulled reversed it can indicate a realization of those things that are blocking us. This is a good sign in cases of illness and addictions. Pulling the Devil card upside down also shows effectively dodging a negative person or situation. This calls for moving forward as you learn from your lessons.

Symbols for the Devil card- Illustration breakdown

- **Devil-** The lack of enlightenment, the Devil represents evil intentions and being a slave to your darkest desires. Half

goat-half man, the Baphomet has bat wings and seems to lord over the other figures illustrated in the card from his position on a pedestal.
- **Inverted Pentagram-** this symbol represents the corruption of virtue and power. The upside-down star is a symbol of Lucifer.
- **Chains-** Symbolic of developing addictions to our own fears and desires. The chains limit freedom, and the figures in the card are being held captive.
- **Torch-** The torch that the Devil holds in the left hand shows ignorance or lack of knowledge. It's also a symbol of enslavement.
- **Figures-** Both nude, there is a male and female figure depicted with chains around their necks. The male has a tail with fire at the end that indicates an addiction to power. The female has a bowl of grapes at the end of her tail showing addiction to the finer things in life. These figures mirror those found in the Lovers card. Their individual power has been stripped from them along with their clothing and they are exposed and ashamed.
- **Block-** The figures are chained to a block of stone that represent having concerns about the material world prevents us from spiritual awareness and enlightenment.

Keywords

Impulse, Materialism, Deception, Sexuality, Anger, Hedonism, Instinct, Forbidden

Reversed Keywords

Release, Weakness, Revelation, Recovery, Blindness, Independence

The Tower

The Tower, the sixteenth card of the Major Arcana, is a call to destroy the lies in our lives. Destroy them so completely that we are left to rebuild things out of the rubble it leaves behind. This card represents the structure of lies and the lightning flash of truth. When something is cleverly constructed, it can take an aggressive act to bring down those beliefs. This is necessary to have the ability to discover the truth. This card signifies that these false structures and institutions in our lives have come or are going to come down suddenly and shockingly. This can be a scary prediction but keep in mind that nothing that is built on falsehood can remain standing. Once this destruction happens, it's able to rebuild on that truth or abandoned altogether.

This card typically signifies destruction on the physical scale rather than spiritual. This isn't necessarily a negative card as change is a normal part of life to embrace. The Tower signifies a time to keep positive and be on the lookout for new insights and understandings that can come to you in a flash. Think of this collapse as cathartic. As an opening of change and communication, this destruction is liberating.

Upright

Also known as "The Liberator," the Tower card can destroy your belief in what you thought you wanted. Many times, this manifests as a personal crisis that forces you to rethink everything in your life. In almost all regards, the Tower card in a spread indicates that your life will be changed.

The Tower tells us that it appears to eliminate that which never fit for us in the first place. This flash of brilliance doesn't come often, but you will know when it does. Once you've crawled out from underneath the rubble you can move forward wiser and stronger. Leave your certainties and go into unchartered territories.

- **Finance and career-** The Tower card urges us to be prepared and to not put everything in one place. You may lose your job or experience a crisis related to financial ruin, but these changes will be for the better no matter how unwelcome they are right now.
- **Love-** Regarding love, The Tower indicates huge change. Though this change can be positive, it will inevitably be stressful for you as it's something that will be unexpected. Your current relationship will be tested and pushed to its limits. Indicating the end of a relationship, or divorce, you must be honest and open with your partner if you wish for the relationship to move forward. When single it can represent assault or violence and warns to be vigilant and mindful.

- o **Health-** The Tower can indicate illness or trauma. It can show a period of illness followed by one of renewal. If you need to make lifestyle changes regarding ongoing health issues, then you need to do so immediately. When this card is pulled regarding health, you must take care to give yourself space to heal or to end behaviors that are destructive.

Reversed Reading

When the Tower is pulled in reverse it can indicate a crisis on the horizon. It can show a struggle against it coming to fruition. The Tower guides us to understand that we need these breakdowns to end our reliance on falsehoods. Allow yourself to be humbled by the destruction and use the end of the deception to bring you peace.

The Tower reversed can also show a narrow escape from a disaster. Maybe you are having a hard time moving on after a tragic event. This is a call for you to externalize that strife that is internal. It can also be interpreted as you attempting to rebuild what has been destroyed with the same pieces that were used to build it before. This urges us to make a fresh start by letting go of the past.

Symbols for The Tower- Illustration breakdown

- **Lightening-** Indicating wrath from above striking down on a tower built by man
- **Fire-** destructive, and consuming everything in its wake
- **Falling People-** Tumbling from the destroyed structure, these people represent the tearing down of what they've known
- **Tower-** Representing a prison of our Spirit, the Tower itself gives a false sense of safety. It's built out of selfish certainty and pride, and its destruction must happen to reveal these deceptions and welcome something new.
- **Windows-** Three windows representing the states of being mental, intellectual, and physical. These windows have fire coming out of them and show that our understanding of the three planes of existence is collapsing.

Keywords

Upheaval, Disaster, Chaos, Revelation, Divorce, Shock, Breakdown, Ruin

Reversed Keywords

Resistance, Fear, Avoidance, Averting Disaster, Delay

The Star

The Star, seventeenth in the Major Arcana, is a card of Hope. It's an indication that you've come through a very difficult time in your life and that you have developed a sense of your own power and resilience. The Star reminds us that we can view all our possible futures in the distance and that if we can focus on one, we can receive guidance towards the realization of it. She begs that we follow that Star and hold onto Hope. This is a card that restores our Faith. It's a guiding light to show us the way.

This card signifies sustenance, and that assistance can come to us in all sorts of places. We must have patience and keep sight of what it is we most want to achieve. This helps us to evaluate those things that are most important to us because we determine if it's worth waiting for. The Star makes us ask what we will carry hope for, what we will go the distance for. We must remember that the Star shows us the things that are possible in the future. Right now, she indicates a space for healing and nurturing. It's up to us to decide what we are going to go for.

Upright

When the Star is drawn in a spread, it's a positive sign for your spiritual life. It calls us to take time to balance our energies and take time for recovery and alignment. The Star urges us to believe in our dreams because anything and everything can happen. This is a sign of hope for the future. A sign of Inspiration and contentment. This is a sign that everything is going to be okay. The star ushers in creativity and allows us to take center stage with our talents. This can mean a period of visualization so that you can manifest what you desire. It interprets into having the stars within your reach.

The Star is the realization of who we are at our core. It's ushering in a calm, peaceful phase in life that provides deep understanding and stability for yourself and those around you. This is a sign that you are now ready to accept the gifts the universe has for you. She is the quiet after the storm, the ultimate peace.

- **Finance and career**- The Star is a great sign for opportunities. It can also show a need to examine finances and shine a light into areas that may have issues. If financial help comes your way, accept it.
- **Love-** Any issues you may have been experiencing should start to mend. The Star advises us to be honest with who we are and to share that in our relationships. Get out and meet new people like the one you are seeking may be in a new crowd.
- **Health-** If you are having feelings of exhaustion, or pressure then you need to take time for your well-being physically, emotionally, and mentally. Typically, a good sign regarding Health, the Star card indicates well-being and healing.

Reversed Reading

When the Star is pulled in a reversed position it can indicate hopelessness and despair. Even if the situation you are facing is not that bad, the fact that you have lost hope makes it hopeless. This can be problems from the past still exhausting us. It calls for a change in attitude regarding the situation in question. The Star upside down begs that you do not play the victim in your circumstances but rather expect that things are going to not only be okay but also that it will be better than you could have hoped for. Have faith that the Divine is always with us and realize that it never left us.

The reversed Star can indicate a test of faith and learning how to trust in yourself. This card calls us to reconnect to that which is most important to us and to discover our soul's purpose in this existence. Keep your mind and eyes open for signs of inspiration as the answers you seek will be provided to you. The energy of the Star reversed is one of nourishment and self-care on a spiritual and deeply personal level. When our energy levels are depleted, we must recognize when to stop pushing ourselves and find the retreat needed to reconnect to our inner essence.

Symbols for The Star- Illustration breakdown

- **Eight-Pointed Star-** In the Spiritual realm, the eight-pointed star represents Purity of the Soul.
- **Seven Stars-** Representing the visible planets, these stars symbolize the influences of the Sun, Moon, Mercury, Venus, Mars, Jupiter, and Saturn.
- **Tree/Bird-** Known as symbolizing the bird of Hermes, this represents a connection between Heaven and Earth.
- **Water-** Spiritual energy and pristine life are represented. The woman has one foot in the water representing her intuition and listening to her inner voice. The container that's pouring water into the small pool lands in five rivulets or rings that symbolize the five senses.
- **Jugs-** Two containers representing the subconscious and the conscious are being poured out. The water that is poured out onto the Earth provides nourishment and continues the cycle of fertility.
- **Naked Woman-** The woman is shown naked representing vulnerability and her purity. She is connected to all living things and is the spiritual manifestation of the Feminine.

Keywords

Hope, Infinity, Faith, Purity, Tranquility, Serenity, Joy

Reversed Keywords

Despair, Illness, Arrogance, Boredom, Depression

The Moon

The Moon card represents the shadow of our Psyche. The eighteenth card, it can be a call to become aware of situations that induce fear and anxiety. The Moon card can reveal hidden truths and a need to search for those forces in our lives that need to be unraveled. This is a time for dealing with memories that we have pushed down or suppressed to not have to deal with them. This card guides us to connect with ourselves on a subconscious level to identify and process those emotions and feelings that we have kept within us.

Because the Moon is associated with Illusion, this card can point to a time where nothing is as what it seems. This leads us to trust our intuition so that we can find all the information needed to decide. The Moon card asks that we use our dreams and inner guidance to control our understanding through the messages we receive.

Upright

The Moon is a powerful card for connecting with the Divine Feminine. This is a time for visualization and intuition to see what lies beneath. It's a time to take note of the lunar cycle and set intentions on the New Moon so that those opportunities can grow. It's a time for honoring your achievements on the Full Moon and identifying those things that you need to release in your life so that you can make space for the good.

When you see the Moon card appear in a spread it can indicate a time of strange events or feelings of oddness. This can be accompanied by strong impulses and psychic visions. The Moon represents deceptions that are hidden and our subconscious communication.

A magical card that reveals mysteries and gives us the ability to create

- **Finance and career-** The Moon card in relation to finances can advise of unknown factors. This could represent coworkers or an authority figure hiding information from you or harboring jealousy. This card comes as a sign to think carefully about what you do and say and to measure facts before making decisions.
- **Love-** Again, the Moon card advises us to consider facts before making decisions and to avoid them until you are certain. This card asks that you trust your intuition and if you have feelings that something is not right, that you should trust that feeling.
- **Health-** There could be issues you are not yet aware of. These can point to mental health issues, menstruation issues in women, and other disorders with addiction. Give yourself the ease of mind by getting any deeded exams.

Reversed Reading

The Moon reversed can indicate that you are experiencing unhappiness or confusion. You may not know the best way to move forward and you may feel unsure of yourself. In this reversed position the Moon card can also show that confusion is starting to fade away. It can be a positive sign that you are effectively handling anxieties. This can be liberation and discovery of positive aspects.

When this card is reversed you may be having a hard time interpreting messages that you are being given. It can be a call to listen to that inner guidance and not external voices. It's a call to trust that you already contain all the answers within you and that subconscious messages are being sent.

When you see the Moon card upside down in a reading, it can point to something you lost making its way back to you. Difficult times that you have been dealing with are coming to an end and your path can be followed with confidence. This card also brings in the answers that you may have been waiting for.

Symbols for The Moon- Illustration breakdown

- **Moon-** As a symbol, it represents the renewal of nature and the feminine. The moon controls the ebb and flow in life, and monthly cycles.
- **Rays-** The rays coming from the Moon are indicative of the Tree of Life.
- **Night-** The night sky symbolizes the unconscious and the dark side of consciousness. This also shows the sleep of Reason.
- **Towers-** Seen as dividing the year into two parts and symbolizing the Solstices of Winter and Summer, or the gates.
- **Dogs-** Thought to symbolize Illusion and Intuition and their duality.
- **Crawfish/Lobster-** Symbolizing a bottom feeder that is on a journey to prove it's worth. This represents the constructs of our minds taking shape and becoming real. The crawfish reminds us that regardless of what others perceive as our worth, it's perseverance that leads to success.
- **Road-** Leading to deeper mysteries, this path represents a road of initiation.

Keywords

Cycles, Vision, Strangeness, Tension, Magic, Insight

Reversed Keywords

Truth, Self-Deception, Common Sense

The Sun

The Sun card represents the energy responsible for all life, and joy. The nineteenth card powers the ideas in our minds and the love within our hearts. The Sun contains no shadows and it's connected with righteousness, truth, and justice. The Sun represents our triumphs in life and the desire of living.

Symbolizing masculinity, the Sun card can represent glory, success, and recognition. Representing a spirit of awareness and streaming energy. The Sun is a positive card that brings with its expansion and growth.

Upright

When the Sun card is drawn, you can be experiencing a time of clarity and transparency. This could mean the ushering in of truth and expansion in our lives. The Sun symbolizes our optimism and freedom. It shows that we are bringing light into our lives and the lives of those around us. It's a shining of positive and transformative light onto any secrets and problems you may have had.

The Sun is a card of Enlightenment that comforts us with the knowledge that it's time to enjoy our spiritual journeys as tribulations are over for now. It asks us to trust the Universe to lead the way and celebrate happiness.

- **Finance and career**- As a card that symbolizes material success, the Sun card shows a great time for promotion, raises, and help from unexpected places. Issues you may have been having will come to a resolution and it's a call to use any windfalls wisely.
- **Love-**The Sun indicates a time of unity and happiness in your passionate relationships. Light will be shed on any issues so that you can see them clearly. This is a great sign for taking the next step in your partnership. The

Sun card indicates good pregnancies and children, so take precautions if you are not prepared for them in your life. If single, you may be enjoying your alone time, or find that your true love is right around the corner.
- **Health-** A sign of Vitality. The Sun card shows improving health and that activity in the light of the Sun can work wonders for your mental and physical health. Again, a great sign for pregnancies.

Reversed Reading

When the Sun card is drawn upside down it can be a sign of depression and sadness. This doesn't reflect the situation at hand rather than the feelings you have about it. You could be feeling burnt out or finding that you do not have the support system you thought you had. The feelings you have could be blocking the Sun's light from allowing clarity to be given.

Reversed, the Sun can also show arrogance and egoism. It reminds us to keep realistic goals and means to reach them. It begs that we ask ourselves if we are overconfident or exuding too much light. If we are having a lack of success, we should allow the Sun's light to help us to rebuild ourselves.

Symbols for Sun- Illustration breakdown

- **Sun-** A sign of Truth and Intelligence defeating Ignorance and Falsehoods. A symbol of Masculinity and Energy.
- **Sunflowers-** The flowers show a willingness regarding seeking the light and following it.
- **Wall-** Representing a boundary between the dimensions of self-awareness and ignorance.
- **Child-** A naked child with raised arms shows innocence and simplicity.
- **Horse-** The Sun card shows a white horse, typically with its head bowed. This symbolizes a connection with the natural world, and of man being in harmony with his higher self.
- **Banner-** Typically shown in Orange, or Red, the Banner represents Vitality, Action, and Movement. The Color also shows Creativity and Power.

Keywords

Energy, Brilliance, Honesty, Radiance, Evolution, Expansion, Optimism

Reversed Keywords

Ego, Pessimism, Sadness, Depression, Unrealistic Expectations

Judgement

The twentieth card of the Major Arcana represents an awakening of Consciousness. The Judgement card is known to represent one responding to a call from a Higher Order. As with the rapture in Christianity, the Judgement card is a call to a time of Sorting. This represents being born again through transformation.

Whether the resolution is good or bad, the time for it is now. This signifies the end of waiting and the reward of a new opening. Sometimes appearing as a messenger, Judgement is calling you for something big. An Enlightenment to open yourself up to and accept.

Judgement represents a huge wakeup call stating that things will never be the same again.

Upright

Pulling the Judgement card advises that it's time for us to reveal the truth. It urges us to act on what we have learned from our previous experiences. It warns us against attempting to conceal the truth as Judgement is fair.

Seeing the Judgement card lets us know our lives have been changed and the transformation is already taking place. Allow yourself to be vulnerable to the call and to be fearless in this transition. You will live at a higher level.

Judgement can also signify a feeling of homesickness, of reuniting with someone close to you, or a homecoming.

- **Finance and career**- Judgement can show that you are being tested or indicate a time of evaluation. Trust that you will get what you deserve and that things will be better for you in the end. This could relate to being fired or receiving a promotion. It's a call to analyze our

spending and make well-thought out decisions regarding finances.
- **Love-** This can be a sign that you are judging your partner too harshly, or they are doing the same to you. It asks that we do not blame each other but work to analyze our feelings. Judgement asks that we rethink the ways we are going about love or finding love.
- **Health-** Judgement asks what ways we might be lying to ourselves regarding our health and well-being. If we take the proper actions, we can improve, and it can also signify a time of healing after an illness.

Reversed Reading

Judgement reversed can indicate letting our fears to hold us from making correct decisions. It can mean that we're wasting time and that opportunities are passing us by. It can also show us denial of lessons and the way that we repeat our mistakes.

This card upside down advises that we do not focus on where we fall short, but to look beyond while taking responsibility for ourselves. Keep in mind that when reversed, Judgment may be a sign that others are gossiping about you or that you are taking the blame for things that you were not involved with. It can also show a time where legal matters were resolved in an unfair way in our lives.

Symbols for Judgement- Illustration breakdown

- **Angel-** The angel in this card shows that we cannot deny the truth and the higher order
- **Cloud**- Representing the unknown, and the way that it's impossible to know everything.
- **Cross-** A cross is depicted as hanging from the Angel's horn symbolizing the cosmic order and balance of opposites.
- **Horn-** This signifies the communication of a message. Literally, the wakeup call that we must respond to.
- **People**-Typically there is a Man, Woman, and Child among other naked figures. They are harkening to the call of the Angel and symbolize the body, mind, and soul.

- **Tomb-**The figures are standing with their feet in tombs, a symbol of resurrection from death.

Keywords

Resurrection, Emergence, Rebirth, Absolution, Revelation

Reversed Keywords

Ignorance, Gossip, Victim, Denial, Self-Doubt

The World

The twenty-first, and last card of the Major Arcana. The World shows the harmonious union of all things. The World card shows us that we can reach beyond the human limitations we have and touch the Divine. It embodies perfection, manifestation, and completion.

In the World card we find the Tetramorph once again represented, but this time they have found their place. This is an indication of success and a resolution to problems. The World gives us a moment of transcendence, a time to revel in our successful living and intuitive listening.

Upright

The World indicates Euphoria. It asks that we take pride and a sense of accomplishment in ourselves. It's telling us that the world is ours for the taking. It's an arrival and the springing up of magic around us.

When the World card appears upright, it's showing that at this moment we do not need anything above what we have at this moment. The integration you've been going through is complete now. This is not a time to be lazy, however, but allow ourselves to take a much-needed rest.

New chapters are coming so take the time to bask in the glory you find around yourself. The World card advises us to become a person that shares the karmic knowledge we have gained and to mentor those around us. This is your sign that you have reached the next level, and that you are ready to move forward.

- **Finance and career-** The World regarding career can signify a time that you will get the recognition you deserve. It's a great time for promotions and being ready to move onward and upward. You may experience financial stability or reward yourself with a vacation or respite.
- **Love-** A positive symbol for relationships, the World can show stability and happiness in relationships as well as a call to relocate those loved ones lost. It is a sign that you're done the inner work needed to find a good partnership. Regarding Love, the World can show meeting someone while on travels, or someone traveling into your life.
- **Health-**a Sign of full recovery, the World is a great sign for health-related matters.

Reversed Reading

When the World card appears reversed it may be a sign of stagnation. Perhaps you've wasted energy on the wrong pursuits or attempted to take shortcuts when the hard way was necessary. Most times you will already know what the problem you are stuck in is.

Reversed, the World card begs that we try another tactic, or stop doing that which is not working for us. It may mean that we have somehow missed the point, or that we're not ready to move outside of our comfort zones. It's representative of a time to cut our losses and move forward.

Symbols for The World- Illustration breakdown

- **Evangelists-**The Tetramorph, shown in the corners of the card represents order and meaning of the Universe.
- **Garland-**Surrounding the figure, the garland represents the crown of glory in life. This surrounds and protects the figure and animals.

- **Woman-**Representing the soul of the world she is dancing and shows the joy of creation as well as the harmony of heaven.
- **The wands-**the naked female figure is holding a candle in each hand that is burning from both ends. This expresses the elements and the complex Universe.

Keywords

Arrival, Finality, Wholeness, Fulfillment, Ending

Reversed Keywords

Burden, Stagnation, Disappointment, Lack of Achievement

CHAPTER 4

Intro To The Minor Arcana

Now that you are familiar with the Major Arcana, the Minor Arcana can be used to gain further insight from them. While these minor cards hold their own interpretations and significance, the correlations and supplementary denotations will help you develop a sense of them in the bigger picture. As you did with the Major cards, spend time with each individual card to see what impressions you pick up and what their significance is to you. Most decks now will include full illustrations on the Minor cards, but some of the more traditional Tarot decks feature simply a symbol or "pips" repeated. The meaning of a Minor card can be determined by its Suit and the position of it within the Suit and in relation to other cards in a spread. While the imagery found in most decks will help with further meaning and correlations, for now, let's look at developing a basic understanding of each card simply as a suit, and a number within a suit. Each card's significance will be determined by several factors including the people involved in the reading, and the questions being asked.

This Arcana consists of 56 cards broken down into four suits of fourteen cards. They are quite like the suits of a regular deck of playing cards but with one additional card. Each suit correlates to an element and some believe a chakra as well. The four Suits are Coins, Wands, Swords, and Cups. They represent the social classes of ancient times they originated in and it's interesting to take note of how they correlate to today's world.

In each Suit, the cards start with the Ace as number one card. They then progress with numbers 2 through 10. We then find the Court Cards: Page/Princess, Knight/Prince, Queen, and King.

The Minor Arcana is just as important as the Major, and they represent those things such as day to day life and relationships. When it comes to the four Minor Arcana Suits, think of them as having a temporary influence. The situations they represent can be changed easily by our actions. These cards can show reflections of thoughts, experiences, emotions, and interactions we experience. If you have a reading with mostly Minor cards it can signify a focus on a fleeting day to day issues and the need to learn from them to focus on the long-term. When there is one more Major Arcana presented with them, they are directly correlating the larger lesson through everyday actions.

The Four Suits of the Minor Arcana

Coins/Pentacles

The Coin cards, or Pentacles, deal with the external or physical level of consciousness. This Suit of the Minor Arcana represents the working class, those that must think about how they will afford the things in life they want. This Suit corresponds to Earth astrological signs and the Earth element. This Suit correlates to the Suit of Diamonds. Other associations are the Root Chakra and the season of Winter. For the most part, Coins symbolize dependability, reliability, and humbleness. This can be reflected in outer situations that show how we create and transform our surroundings. Also associated with self-image, Coins include the material aspects in our lives.

Seeing the Coin Suit in readings can indicate manifestation or a realization of situations in your life. It can show that you are seeking ways to fix problems and concerns with material conflicts. On the flipside, they can advise of freed, and over-indulgence. These cards are reflective of the abundance we have in our lives. An imbalance regarding this aspect of our lives can create detachment, anxiety, and insecurity. We can use the guidance of the Coins to meet our needs and gain clarification on solutions in front of us.

Wands

Also known as Staves, Rods, and Staffs the Suit of Wands is associated with Spring as well as the element of Fire. They correspond to the Suit of Clubs and the Third Chakra or the Solar Plexus Chakra. Wands reflect the growing middle class of the time period. That includes those that owned their businesses and had fewer worries about money and more time was spent on self-improvement and moving forward. When we draw any Wand card it should be considered a call to action. This call to action may require an extra amount of energy from you. Wands refer to a time of change and an urge to make bold moves but in a measured way.

Mainly related to our sense of purpose and careers, Wands are connected to desire and charms so they can aid us and offer guidance as we make these moves. Wands carry ideas and innovations and are relative to our life energy. With the connection to the Fire Element, Wands can be the light that conquers darkness and provide the vitality needed to not only survive but to thrive. When interpreted negatively the Wand cards represent egotistical behavior and a lack of direction or purpose. The Suit of Wands can give great insight into our resilience and able to go the distance in a given situation.

Swords

Associated with the Air element, Swords as a suit symbolize our mental consciousness. Air is known for its constant movement and for being cleansing and powerful. While remaining unseen, it is the power and knowledge for change. The Suit of Swords also correlates to the season of Autumn, and the Heart or Fourth Chakra. Swords represent the upper class, even royalty. They indicate the quality of our thoughts and beliefs. A double-edged sword can show the existence between power and intellect and the need to balance them with feeling and spirit.

When Sword cards are drawn, they are in association with the change, ambition, and even oppression. They can be interpreted as either having destructive or constructive expressions. Swords tell us to be cautious of what's occurring around us and to seek solutions for the decisions we must make. Sword cards can be tricky to understand because of how complex our minds are and how quickly they can change. Develop your intuition with this Suit so that you can distinguish their deeper, sometimes hidden, positive messages.

Cups

Transcending class they are representative of our emotions, feelings, and connections. Associated with the Water element, these cards indicate using your heart when making decisions and the spontaneous reactions we have. Correlating with the Suit of Hearts and the Sacral or Second Chakra. The Suit of Cups is also linked to imagination and creativity, Cups cards show that one is pulling energy from their inner selves.

When read in reverse Cups can represent that we are disengaged or have unrealistic expectations in the situations and people in our lives. It could signify that we are repressing our emotions or that we're disengaged. Like Water can be soft yet formative, the Cups urge us to get "in the flow" with ourselves. These cards point to the pleasure, sensuality, and passion that we may or may not have in our lives. Strongly associated with relationships, the Cups incorporate the past, present, and future hints about a situation or person.

CHAPTER 5

Minor Arcana Number Card Relationships

Since each of the Suits have the same number of cards, they are closely associated in the larger picture. When first learning to understand and read the cards, understanding the similarities and differences in each Suit by the numbers.

The Minor Arcana Number associations at a Glance

Aces

Corresponding with the Major Arcana card The Magician. The Aces represent inventive ideas and the independent spirit.

- **Coins-** Producing, Solidity, Small Wins
- **Wands-** Eagerness, New Energies, Efficiency
- **Swords-** Resolve, Discoveries, Clarity
- **Cups-** Intense Emotions, Love, New Relationships

Twos

Corresponding to the High Priestess, the Two's symbolize Choice and Cooperation

- **Coins-** Strewn, Jumbled, Juggling. Trouble balancing.
- **Wands-** Opening, Choice, Success. Opportunity.
- **Swords-**trucc, Hard Choice, Deadlock. The internal struggle for balance.
- **Cups-**Meeting, Compatibility, Partnership. Coming together of people.

Threes

The Empress correspondents, the Three's are our Creativity and Self-Expression

- **Coins-** Asset, Networking, Mastery

- **Wands-** New Energy, Productivity, Enthusiasm
- **Swords-** Pain, Despair, Conflict
- **Cups-** Togetherness, Copiousness, Obligation

Fours

Corresponds to the Emperor. The Four's represent Discipline and Order

- **Coins-** Closed, Stability, Miserliness
- **Wands-** Thrill, Celebration, Togetherness
- **Swords-** Observation, Rest, Research
- **Cups-** Daze, trivial Loss, Self-Absorbed

Fives

The Hierophant Major Arcana is associated with the Five's. These are cards of Exploration and Curiosity.

- **Coins-** Holdup, Loss, Hard Times
- **Wands-** Opposition, Strain, New Business
- **Swords-** Companion, Synchronization, Excursion
- **Cups-** Regret, Forfeiture, Crash

Sixes

Corresponding with the Lovers, the Sixes are representative of Harmony and Peace

- **Coins-** Help, Kindness, Accepting Help
- **Wands-** Triumph, Recognition, Festivity
- **Swords-** Companion, Journey, Concord
- **Cups-** Sentimentality, Reminiscence, Old Friends

Sevens

The Chariot correspondents. The Seven's are our Ambition and Enthusiasm

- **Coins-** Waiting, Idea, Time will Tell
- **Wands-** Defiance, Contest, Under Siege
- **Swords-** Hidden, Deception, Theft

- **Cups**-Illusion, Fantasy, Indecisiveness

Eights

The Eight's correspond to the Strength card representing Power and Strength

- **Coins-** Arrogance, Spiritual Peace, Workmanship
- **Wands- Activity, Change, Movement**
- **Swords**-Pain, Isolation, Trapped
- **Cups**-Journey, Moving, Abandonment

Nines

Corresponds to the Hermit. This is a representation of Spiritual Strength and Inner-Knowledge

- **Coins-** Indulgence, Luxury, Happiness
- **Wands-** Protection, Guard, Overextending
- **Swords**-Worrying, Agony, Reflection
- **Cups**-Accomplishment, Fulfilment, Indulgence

Tens

The Wheel of Fortune of the Major Arcana, the Ten's symbolize the end of a cycle and represent new luck and opportunities.

- **Coins-** Family, Money, Fortune
- **Wands-** Weight, Overcommitting, Tension
- **Swords**-Ending, Treachery, Fate
- **Cups**-Joy, Family, Peace

CHAPTER 6

Minor Arcana Court Card Relationships

The Minor Arcana Court Card associations at a Glance

The Pages

These are enthusiastic and delightful cards with themes of vitality, learning, and youth. The Page sees the world through new eyes and it's easy for them to find new inspiration in the natural world. Each Page holds the symbols of their respective Suit as they are drawn to the meanings of those symbols. They focus on learning everything there is to know about them, as they want to experience everything they can. Symbolic of our instinctual interests and ability to see the magic in our surrounding world.

- **Coins**

Brings the Eagerness to the practical world. This can manifest in new plans for business, training or entrepreneurial interests. The Page of Coins wants to make a direct impact and work towards stability.

- **Wands**

Brings the Power of Creativity when uniting the energy of the Pages. This represents the development of new creative skills and the interest in learning by doing.

- **Swords**

The Page of Swords represents increasing interests in Intellectual pursuits and the collection of new information. They have a strong motivation and loves facts and figures.

- **Cups**

This Page is sensitive and seeks out new connections and feelings. This can signify a need to connect with our spirituality and inner guidance.

The Knights

These cards in the Minor Arcana are the hands-on adventurers that represent risk-taking and irrational decision making. Even though their hasty choices can bring consequences or setbacks, the Knights bring a high level of energy to any situation. They help us find the push you need to get things going and the passion to inspire others. They have no time for abstractions or concepts, they want to learn by doing and will dive straight into any task given to them.

- **Coins**

The most down to earth of the Knights. The Knight of Coins is practical and takes deliberate action. They must be completely certain that the path they are on is what they want. They make plans a reality.

- **Wands**

One of the most charismatic cards of the entire Tarot, the Knight of Wands pairs that Fiery energy of the Suit with the desire to jump in and get things done.

- **Swords**

This Knight is about testing ideas. He explores how we can communicate thoughts and principles. The Knight of Swords is cerebral and generally well meaning.

- **Cups**

The Knight of Cups is a romantic that uses art and imagery to meet challenges. He will not accept anything less than perfect, which can make him withdrawn but able to sweep anyone off their feet.

The Queens

A powerful Archetype that is interested in expressing their power creatively. They are curious about their Suits and can reference periods of power and openness. Queens are in tune with themselves and are dynamic, able to be flexible with the world around them. When we see Queens in a reading, they ask how we are using our abilities, and help lead us to personal satisfaction and the support of others.

- **Coins**

The Queen of Coins has a deep connection to the Natural World. She values the deeper meaning and using her resources to

help others. She has built a life of decadence and lives the life she wants.
- **Wands**

Vivacious and charming, this Queen is dependable and creative. The Queen of Wands is fiercely independent and overly charismatic.
- **Swords**

Has formidable intellect and has a powerful understanding of the world. She is a trusted advisor as she revels in learning more about her world and trusts her perceptions.
- **Cups**

The Queen of Cups is a natural healer who works in connections and emotions. She is receptive and caring and holds the pace for others and herself. She awakens Spirituality in others.

The Kings

The Kings of the Minor Arcana deal with questions of leadership and authority. They have mastered their Suit with dedication and practice, and they are confident and determined.

- **Coins**

Formidable yet joyous in leadership. The King of Coins lives in abundance and values celebration and using his wealth for himself and others. He has an unmatched command of resources.
- **Wands**

A Pioneer of new ideas and a noticeable leader. The King of Wands values creativity and innovation. He is motivated by change and can be careless about the feelings of others.
- **Swords**

More of an Intellectual, the King of Swords deals in concepts and planning. This abstract thinking reflects his intelligence that inspires others.
- **Cups**

Dealing with Emotions and the dynamics of our personal relationships, this King inspires those big picture questions and our intuition.

CHAPTER 7

Techniques For Reading Tarot

When you are ready to start practicing spreads, find a few that you are most comfortable with. You only need simple spreads that use a few cards when first starting out. Even the most advanced Tarot readers still find benefit from a three-card spread.

Begin by clearing your cards of energy and shuffling them thoroughly. With any spreads, you'll want to meditate on your question while shuffling. Continue shuffling the cards as you repeat your question until you feel ready to lay them down.

Feel free to cut the deck as many times as you want or have the person you are reading for shuffle and cut them. Find a ritual that gets you in the best head space to analyze and interpret the images you are about to see. You may feel the need to use a "clarifying card." This is when you pull an additional card to provide more context to a spread. You don't want to use this as a crutch, but it can be used when more information is needed.

If you have a friend that's able to help you, try doing this exercise to improve your contrast and comparison abilities. You can use this method of practicing for focusing on the entire deck, the Major Arcana by itself, or the Minor Arcana independently. In any case, you'll start by shuffling the deck. Once shuffled, take the top card and put it in front of you to the right. This is the card for your friend. Then take the next card and place it slightly to the left of the first, as the card that represents what happens to yourself. Perform a mini-reading. Do this again with the next two cards and work your way through the entire deck. This will increase your familiarity with the cards and get you used to look at all the cards equally. We need to remember that these cards are all equal and that we should have any reservations with drawing certain cards. Also, try to come up with different impressions and meanings instead on one rigid definition of each card. Don't spend too much time on any card or pair of cards. You can ask a simple question before each draw, or you can simply perform this exercise to simply create your own stories for the cards.

For even further insight into the relationship of the cards in a spread, pay attention to if they are facing one another or if they are facing away from each other. What type of indications comes up when we take note of the way the figures in the cards are facing? Look through your cards and find figures in each card that are looking towards or away from each other.

Ask yourself the following questions:

- What's the purpose of this interaction?
- Is the subject matter positive or negative?
- Why might they be facing away from each other, or facing each other regarding this scenario or question?
- What are these cards communicating?
- Are they ignoring each other?

Spreads

One Card

As mentioned before, you can simply pull one card a day. Set your intention before you pull the card by asking what energy you need to focus on, or what you might experience in your day. Make a note about what card you drew and what stood out to you about it. At the end of the day, journal any correlations you found.

Three Card Spreads

- Past-Present-Future

Many Three Card spreads relate to the Past, Present, and Future. Place the cards left to right and they will represent the past, present, and future positions. You can find the things that shaped who you are and what's happening in your life now as well as receive an indication of where the energy in your life is leading. Keep in mind that your current actions have the power to change everything.

- Blessings- Challenges- Action

Another Three Card Spread is the Blessings, Challenges, Action spread. If you are seeking clarity regarding the next step, then this spread can be beneficial. Laid the same way as the Past, Present, and Future spread, this shows where you will find help in this situation in the Blessings position. For Challenges, you see what problem you need to solve, or what you're up against. With the Action position, it signifies what you should or should not do to address the challenge.

- Situation- Action- Outcome

In unclear situations, this three-card spread can be particularly helpful. The left card, the Situation, is the thing you've asked about. This may look different than you expected but it will give insight into what's going on. The middle card, the Action card, is a recommendation of the action needed to get to the card on the right, the Outcome card.

Five Card Spread

1. The far-left position, or the bottom, represents the reasons leading to the situation at hand.
2. The left of center position reveals those things in our past that still affect us currently.
3. The center position represents our present situation.
4. This position signifies our future outcomes.
5. The top card is possible outcomes if the course of action is followed.

Celtic Cross Spread

One of the most popular spreads, the Celtic Cross uses 10 cards in a circle/line layout. There are many variations regarding how the cards are laid but they will typically consist of five cards (one in the middle and four cards surrounding it – one on each side of the middle card and one card laid sideways on the center card.). Then a line to the right of those five for cards seven through ten.

1. Center card on the bottom. The first card you lay. It represents the current condition.
2. Center card laid on top of Card #1. Represents your Current Obstacles and Troubles.
3. Above the center card, representing the best outcome possible.
4. To the Right of the center card, representing the cause for the current situation.

5. Below the center card, representing your near past.
6. To the Left of the center card, representing you in the near future.
7. On the Bottom of the Line to the right of the circle. This card represents in general, who you are right now and your relation to the theme of the question.
8. Directly above the preceding card, this position represents your current surroundings as it relates to your question. (environment, family, friends)
9. Directly above the preceding card, representing fears and hopes regarding the situation or your life in general if there is no specific question.
10. The final and top card of the line, this card represents the outcome, or how this phase is turning out.

Horseshoe Spread

A seven card spread where there is one main card placed in the center and has three cards laid on either side of it forming a staggered version of a horseshoe. This spread is read from left to right.

1. The Past (The first card on the bottom left working towards the Center and down the right side)
2. The Present
3. Hidden Influences
4. You, or the Querent
5. Attitudes of others
6. What you should do
7. The Outcome

There are so many spreads for you to learn, and multiple variations on each one that you should have plenty to practice with. Find which spreads you are comfortable with. You can use certain spreads for certain types of questions, or for deeper understanding in the cards relationships.

You may decide to include reverse cards in your readings, or not. Don't feel pressured to do anything you're not ready to commit to!

The Fool's Journey

When developing a greater connection with the Tarot, you may want to start with "The Fool's Journey." Picture yourself as the

Fool and we will travel through each of the cards of the Major Arcana. This can help you build those associations you will rely upon when performing readings. This exercise is a great way to view the cards objectively. Using The Fool's Journey to practice learning the Tarot will also help you understand the personality and energies of each archetype.

On this journey, the Fool gets more enlightened as they travel.

1. **The Fool-** The hero of our story into the Major Arcana. There is so much excitement for the coming Divine journey that we don't always watch our step and we have no awareness of the risks coming our way.

2. **The Magician-** He teaches the Fool and ignites his inquisitiveness. All possibilities are laid out in the form of tools from each Suit, and the Fool sees all the directions they can take. The Fool wonders if the Magician had these tools already or if they were created just then.

3. **The High Priestess-** Another teacher who begs the Fool to use their intuition before getting into situations. She's the opposite of the Magician, being quiet and still. She hands the Fool ancient scrolls and they find that through introspection they have decided which action or path they will pursue.

4. **The Empress-** A mother figure and creator. She advises the Fool that this path will require patience and that they will need to develop a way to manage this new creation. She impresses the need for time to mature and loving attention.

5. **The Emperor-** A father figure that shows the Fool the importance of discipline and authority. The Fool is amazed at how the Emperor is obeyed and finds that strong will and braveness will help them manage their quest. The Fool is now ready to lead and heads away from the Emperor with a new purpose.

6. **The Hierophant-** Shows the importance of Tradition to the Fool. The Fool realizes the fear they have regarding what they have built. The Hierophant begs the Fool to consider

all options and understand the legacy of what has been gained thus far. The Fool is at ease as he heads away on his journey.

7. **The Lovers-** The Fool encounters the Lovers between the current path they are on and new love. They decide between continuing down the path they were already on and deciding to take this new Love hey have found along with them. The Fool makes the choice to choose Love and heads down a whole new road.

8. **The Chariot-** Teaches the Fool to keep the course and make up their mind so that victory is inevitable. The Fool eventually loses faith in the journey and allows enemies and circumstances, even their own confusion to delay and derail them. The Charioteer advises the Fool to put on their armor, make a decision regarding their resolve, and to run over anything standing in the way. The Fool understands that victory is only the beginning.

9. **Strength-** This is the figure that shows the Fool quiet confidence and power. The Fool leaves the Charioteer feeling arrogant and powerful. They come across Strength closing the mouth of a lion and they want to connect to the higher energy that was used. Strength advises the Fool to direct their passions to get more out of them.

10. **The Hermit-** Encourages the Fool to think introspectively of all the lessons learned so far. After the lessons learned from Strength, the Fool needs time to retreat. Meeting the Hermit, the Fool begins to see those hidden areas of their mind. The Fool realizes they have the power to illuminate the darkness.

11. **The Wheel of Fortune-** The Fool sees that nothing is ever the End and that life is repeated cycles. The Fool comes out of hiding with the Hermit and finds that they need a change. The Fool notices how things change by the hour, in a never-ending way. The Fool begins to feel that everything is coming back to them three-fold.

12. **Justice-** The Fool learns to be fair and rational. The Fool finds Justice making a fair decision that benefits both parties even though they do not necessarily see it that way. Justice shows the Fool to realign their inner scales and maintain balance.

13. **The Hanged Man-** The Fool is changed by the experience of being turned upside down and inspecting life from a new perspective. The Fool leaves Justice and spends time under a tree in deep introspection. They awaken and start to hang upside down from the tree and surrenders everything and receives a dazzling moment of realization. With their head full of these visions, the Fool continues.

14. **Death-** The Fool learns the value in death and clearing out the old to bring in the new. The Fool begins to feel sad at the realization that the old ways are gone. Because the old ways and old self were sacrificed, Death took them. The Fool is devastated at the loss but understands it's natural to mourn so that new things have space. As Death leaves, the Fool feels like everything has been stripped away he begins to move again.

15. **Temperance-** The Fool Learns to put two opposites together in the creation of a third, balanced force. The Fool comes across Temperance mixing the contents of their cups together and is amazed to learn that all opposites can create a unified third.

16. **The Devil-** The Fool sees the addictions they have subjected themselves to. As the Fool passes by the mountain they begin to feel desires come back and they rail against them thinking it's a test of spirituality. The Devil advises the Fool that it's simply the things that already exist inside of them that are being realized and that they can be used on the quest. The Fool learns that some use the impulses to reach the highest heights and refuse to find contentment in the obsessions. The Fool leaves understanding this key.

17. **The Tower-** The Fool sees the collapse of everything they previously thought but finds a way to start anew. When the Fool passes the Tower, they remember building it when they had to make a mark on the world and prove themselves. In a flash, the Fool realizes that he is no different from the arrogant people sitting inside the Tower. The Fool understands that he is not singular and superior. The Fool shouts out this realization and the Tower is struck by lightning, reducing it to rubble. The Fool feels profound fear but feels their third eye has opened. The lies in the Fools life are destroyed and he is forced to rebuild on the foundation of truth.

18. **The Star-** The Fool finds a period of quiet healing. The Fool feels lost and is in despair when they come across a woman reflecting starlight holding two urns. She invites the Fool to be rejuvenated and helps to heal their wounded heart. The Fool admires the stars and the woman explains that by focusing on one possible future or start, that they will be guided to their destination.

19. **The Moon-** The Fool learns that most of their troubles are simply illusions of the mind. With renewed Hope, the Fool continues down the path that is now illuminated by the Moon. The Fool realizes they are in a strange land that he believed to be beyond the veil. The Fool sees the boat in the distance and understands that while he can remain in this primal land of mystery, he can also trust himself to the river as the Moon is in control either way. In the boat, the Fool surrenders to the magic of the Moon and sleeps.

20. **The Sun-** The Fool finds a new beginning. When the Fool awakens to the sunrise. A child's laughter is heard, and the Fool watches the child take joy in all the things being discovered. The Fool finds himself smiling and feels light and illuminated. The Fool sees the world in a new light and watches the child turn into the sunlight as he discovers that the child is himself. The Fool realizes that they have met their own inner light. Feeling that they are close to the end of their journey, the Fool proceeds to take the final steps.

21. **Judgement-** The Fool learns to move on and how to forgive themselves. The Fool sees Judgement and finds that there is only one final step to take on this journey but that it cannot be taken until the past is laid to rest. Judgement explains that the only way to get rid of the past that we walk with under our feet is to call it up and comes to terms with it. The Fool is handed a small trumpet and understanding that Judgement is right, he must come to terms with everything that has happened. When the Fool blows the trumpet, the Earth is cracked and all the Fools past selves rise up to be faced. The Fool forgives all these past-selves and reaches an understanding with them. The Fool becomes reborn and returned to living in the present. He takes that final step.

22. **The World-** The Fool understands the world is theirs and that the cycle begins again. The Fool is bemused to find that same cliff they started from when they first began. Seeing this position differently, the Fool understands that everything is entwined, and everything is One. The Fool takes that final step off the cliff and is drawn upward to a place where he can view the entire world. He becomes one with the universe, and the journey begins as it comes to an end.

Sample Reading 1

In this Sample Reading, we will do a Three Card Spread indicating Past, Present, and Future.

The Question we are posing is "How can I improve in my career today?"

The cards laid from left to right are the Five of Cups, the Three of Cups, and the Queen of Cups.

Knowing that Cups represent Emotion, we already know that Emotions are heavily influencing how we (or the querent) conduct business.

Let's break down each card and the position they are in:

1. **First Position- Five of Cups**

We know that the Five's represent Forfeiture and Regret as well as Exploration. This tells us that the Five of Cups represents crying over spilt milk. It shows us not having a good attitude, and what we have been indulging in the past.

2. Second Position -Three of Cups
We learned that the Three's show an Obligation, and Togetherness as well as Creativity. This tells us that we need to join forces with others. It can also indicate that we need to make time for a break for reflection.

3. Third Position – Queen of Cups
The Queen of Cups awakens the Spirituality in others and holds space for herself. This can advise us that things are being restored to success once we get our Emotions under control. This shows that the more adjusted you are in your Emotional life, the better your career will be.

Additional Sample Readings

Two Card Share

For this next Sample, we will use the two-card quick pull that we used to introduce ourselves to the cards. Assuming that you have a friend with you begin by shuffling and then each of you cutting the deck. Place the first card in front of yourself, and the second card in front of your friend. In this sample, we won't be asking a question of the deck but using the cards to ask questions of ourselves based on the interpretation of the cards.

1. Your Card-The Chariot. This card brings us to ask what motivates us. What is driving us? What in your life are you fiercely determined to achieve?
2. Friends Card-The Hanged Man. This card has us ask Where we need to make room for Compromise? It also has us ask what in our life is currently "on hold, or stalled?

Reflect on the cards you pull for a moment, take note of any questions or insights that resonate with you and draw again!

Movie Scene Spread

Pull a card and describe the card as a scene in a Movie. Don't bother with your intuition, for now, just name what you see in the card as if it's a scene in a movie. For example, we'll pull The Tower. Ask yourself the following questions regarding The Tower.

- What type of scene is this? Is it a beginning scene, or an action scene? The Tower would strongly resonate with an action scene.
- What is happening in this scene? People are falling out of the tower, things are on fire, and it seems scary.

Pull another card. We'll go with The Queen of Wands:

- What type of scene is this? When you encounter a Court card they are typically just sitting there. Pull a second card to place over it slightly. Now picture the figure from your Court card in the scenario presented in the second card. We pull the Eight of Swords as our second card.
- How does the Queen act as the figure put into the Eight of Swords? The happiness and fertility in the Queen card now

looks like she is in trouble with the connotation of the Eight of Swords.
- Create a summary of this "movie scene: You may describe this as someone falling from grace or someone that got themselves into trouble.

Remember to keep things simple when starting out. The smaller the better at first. There is so much that you can do and explore without things becoming too overwhelming for you in the beginning. Keep your readings practical and keep them short term. Keep your questions simple. Ask the cards what you should focus on today and pull one card for yourself. Pull a Card of Gratitude. Find something in the card you pull that shows you how you can gather gratitude from it and into your life. Pull a card asking What or Who can you embody today? Ask what you need to Release and Receive.

You will begin to learn what the Tarot truly is capable of, and what the cards point to.

CONCLUSION

Thank you, and congratulations on making it through to the end of this book. I hope that it was informative and able to provide you with all the tools you need for beginning your journey into Tarot. The next step is to start trying some of these techniques on your own and discover what works best for you. Tarot is for everyone, but it takes that bold first step to literally harness the power of your own intuition. With practice and determination, you will be able to master the art of psychic Tarot reading and truly understand each card in the Major and Minor Arcana. You will develop your Intuition and build skills and find that you're able to easily interpret the signs being shown to you and anyone you read for.

You should have a basic understanding of the history of the Tarot, and you may be able to see how these cards could have been used in a regular card game. Discover what ways you can play with the cards for entertainment and to gain insight. While we focused on the Minor Arcana as pips, or general representations that are aligned in each suit it's now time to discover the illustrations for these cards.

Take the time to break down each of the Minor Arcana into the descriptions that were provided in this book for the Major cards. Start with one suit and work your way through all of them. This will be extremely beneficial for you regarding giving in-depth readings and understanding the correlations between all the cards in a spread.

You now know how to select a new deck and clean any energies that are still hanging on to it. Using the steps in this book, you can develop a bond with the cards and with each card individually. Understand that it's these relationships to the cards that you will use in reading for yourself and others. Follow the Fool's Journey to dedicate the Major Arcana to memory, and to realize what phases of life you have experienced and could be reflecting right now. Use the practice spreads to see how the information in this book correlates to the practical reading of the cards. Use these basics to form the foundation you use when moving onto more advanced symbolism and interpretations.

Keep a Tarot journal so that you have a dedicated place to keep note of your journey. Make note of cards that speak to you personally. Reflect on your first spreads, and what cards you seem to see repeatedly. Spend time with your reflections every now and then to see how far you've come and consistently add new insights as you move further along in your journey. Remember, these cards represent you. Take the time to get to know yourself better and you will be more aligned with your inner, and higher selves.

Lastly, if you enjoyed this book, I ask that you please take the time to rate it on Amazon. Your honest review would be greatly appreciated. Thank You!

DESCRIPTION

If you are ready to learn how to read Tarot, then this book is for you! Inside you'll find the history behind Tarot Cards and learn about the Symbolism represented in the decks. It doesn't matter if you're an absolute beginner or if you're looking to reconnect to the Tarot that you've known before. There are methods provided to teach you how to not only read the cards as you encounter them, but also to make intuitive interpretations of each card individually as well as in their relation to the rest of the deck.

Tarot started as a card game in the mid-14th Century, and over the years slowly morphed into a tool of Divination. Since that time, Tarot has become a trusted source for personal introspection and guidance. Traditionally shrouded in mystery and even fear, the Tarot has begun to pull away from the negative stigma that is associated with it. In recent years the Tarot has increased in popularity, possibly because of the uncertain times we are living in or because it is a part of a larger trend towards mindfulness. No matter the reason you are drawn to the Tarot, with the information in this book, you can easily learn how to read and use the cards!

We'll explore the 22 cards of the Major Arcana-the "trump" cards of the Tarot deck. These cards represent those life-lessons, or archetypal themes in our lives. The symbology and meanings associated with the Major Arcana can be complex, and in this book you will find complete descriptions of their Illustrations and traditional symbols. We also explore common themes that are asked of the Tarot such as Health, Love, Career & Finance, and Spiritual meanings including keywords to remember.

Next, we introduce the 56 cards of the Minor Arcana-the "minor" cards. These cards of the Tarot represent those day-to-day experiences in life. Represented by numbers or "pips", the Minor Arcana is outlined in four Suits: The Cups, The Swords, The Coins, and The Wands. These cards are found represented by Ace through 10's as well as Court Cards or Page, Knight, Queen, and King. We'll learn how these Minor Arcana cards relate to each other in terms of which Suit they are, and common interpretations for each card.

Finally, you'll find sample spreads and techniques for dealing and reading your Tarot cards. The rewards you will obtain by being able to confidently shuffle and cast cards will be worth the time and effort you put into learning Tarot. One of the most important factors to consider is your reason for wanting to learn Tarot. Use this reason to motivate you to develop a personal relationship with each of the Major cards, and then onto the Minor.

In this book you will discover how to create a connection to the Tarot and develop your skills of intuition as you work with the cards. It's this connection that you will rely upon to form your own opinions and explanations of the readings you provide for yourself and others.

Some of the information included in this book:

- The History of Tarot
- How to choose your first deck and clear energies
- Breakdown of the Major and Minor Arcana
- Introduction to "The Fool's Journey"
- Techniques for Reading Tarot
- Practice Spreads
- Sample Readings
- And much more...

www.ingramcontent.com/pod-product-compliance
Lightning Source LLC
Chambersburg PA
CBHW071503070526
44578CB00001B/432